LOYALTY-BASED SELLING

LOYALTY-BASED SELLING

The Magic Formula for Becoming the #1 Sales Rep

Tim Smith

AMACOM

American Management Association

New York • Atlanta • Boston • Chicago • Kansas City • San Francisco • Washington, D.C.
Brussels • Mexico City • Tokyo • Toronto

Special discounts on bulk quantities of AMACOM books are available to corporations, professional associations, and other organizations. For details, contact Special Sales Department, AMACOM, a division of American Management Association, 1601 Broadway, New York, NY 10019.
Tel.: 212-903-8316.   Fax: 212-903-8083.
Web site: www.amacombooks.org

This publication is designed to provide accurate and authoritative information in regard to the subject matter covered. It is sold with the understanding that the publisher is not engaged in rendering legal, accounting, or other professional service. If legal advice or other expert assistance is required, the services of a competent professional person should be sought.

Grateful acknowledgement is made to the following sources for permission to reference and/or reprint their works and materials:
Day-Timer, Inc., One Day-Timer Plaza, Allentown, PA 18195-1551 (pages 111-118).
HOPE Publications, Kalamazoo, Michigan, (616) 343-0770 (page 89).
Tha Gallup Organization, 301 South 68th Street, Lincoln, NE 68510 (page 44 and page 146).
USA TODAY, copyright 1997 (page 38).
The Guerilla Group, 1002 Walnut, Suite 101, Bolder, CO 80302 (page 44 and page 132).
Franklin Covey Co., 2200 West Parkway Blvd., Salt Lake City, Utah 84119-2099 (pages 111-118).

Library of Congress Cataloging-in-Publication Data

Smith, Tim
    Loyalty-based selling : the magic formula for becoming the #1 sales rep /
    Tim Smith
        p. cm.
    Includes bibliographical references and index.
    ISBN 0-8144-7104-8
    1. Selling. 2. Customer loyalty. I. Title.

HF5438 .S634
658.8'12—dc21

                                                                    2001022195

Printing number

10 9 8 7 6 5 4 3 2 1

CONTENTS

PREFACE

You are a great performer. You wouldn't be reading this if you were content with being average. Like many other superstars, you probably skip the Preface of many books you read because you want to get right to the good stuff. At the same time, you probably feel a tinge of guilt after you skip it. You worry that you have missed a kernel of wisdom that might make you even better.

I can relate directly to your predicament. I feel the same way about Prefaces. Here's a solution. The remainder of this Preface will consist of blank pages. This will allow you to skip it without feeling any guilt.

LOYALTY-BASED SELLING

HOW AND WHO

How Is Loyalty-Based Selling Different?

Sales reps are busy people. Let me qualify that: the best sales reps are busy people. Their schedules are full, and their lives are fast-paced. They have no time to waste.

As a sales rep myself, I am sensitive to this, and that is precisely why this book is to the point, without filler and fluff. Noticeably absent are overused clichés such as "To be successful, you need to focus on achievement instead of activity," "You have to walk the talk," "You should visualize through your mind's eye," and so on.

In this book, there is no more than one example per key point, so you can move fast and learn fast. I respect your time and your intelligence.

Another departure from the standard sales book is the "how-to" versus the "psychosophical" approach—that combination of psychological and philosophical. The standard book discusses the rep's psychology and the customer's to motivate reps into action, and then it reviews in depth the philosophies involved in sales.

Using a sports analogy, the standard book focuses on scoring more points. It attempts to motivate psychologically, but it doesn't give the plays. There are few specifics on what actions to take. You may have a warm and fuzzy feeling after reading it, but that changes nothing tangibly in how you go about your business.

Loyalty-Based Selling is all about the plays. It is a "how-to" book packed with skills and actions. It sets out seven magic steps—concrete actions designed to secure customer loyalty permanently. They are supported with specifics on how to apply them in your job. The results that you will achieve from implementing these steps will fan the flames of your internal motivation. Instead of feeling warm and fuzzy, you will be fueled with ideas and fired up for action.

Incidentally, that will be the last sports analogy of the book. Most sales books are filled with countless sports stories. Don't get me wrong—I am a sports fanatic. I love to watch and play virtually all sports, with the possible exception of rhythmic gymnastics. Nonetheless, even I tire easily from such a one-track focus. I threw in one sports analogy for good measure. There will be no more.

Many books set out strategies designed to improve sales, but the changes required to implement them often can be made only at the CEO level. This book, and its Seven Magic Steps, are targeted to you, the sales rep, because you are the CEO of the sales territory. In essence, you run your own business. You get marketing and manufacturing support from your employer, but you really make the daily decisions that affect your results.

Nonetheless, CEOs and other managers can clearly benefit from reading this book. A company that has all of its sales reps implementing the Seven Magic Steps will blow away its competition. Company leaders at all levels should encourage their reps and all personnel who support customers (even indirectly) to apply these principles.

The supporting examples in this book are positive affirmations, not negative stories. You will not have to suffer through another "The service on that airline was so bad..." story. And all of them come from reps who have been number one in their respective companies.

Finally, most sales books attempt to help you become better. If you find "better" an acceptable goal, please return this book immediately for a refund. But if you accept nothing short of being number one, this is the book for you. I will not hint around at achieving this goal. Rather, I give you a specific plan that will empower you to become the best.

Who Is Tim Smith?

"And why should I listen to him?" This is a valid question. I am not a full-time university professor or Ph.D. consultant. I am not a full-time public speaker. I am just a sales rep.

Although these points might appear to be reasons to question the value of this book, actually these are precisely the factors that give it great value. I am an active sales rep and proud of it. I did the job concurrently as I wrote this book. I can directly relate to all of the sales reps reading this. I am sharing the concepts with you from eye level, one sales rep to another. The information is not coming down to you from high above. The premise is that sales reps learn best from their top-performing peers.

I am much more comfortable writing about the achievements of others rather than my own, but my editor talked me into setting out my revenue growth numbers in my sales territory from the year that I wrote this book. This real-life illustration provides credibility to the example given in the next chapter. In addition, this shows that I practice what I preach. In the year I wrote this book, I literally practiced it as I preached it. I took a half-day out of each sales week to write, time that provided me with a focus on the Seven Magic Steps, which, as you will now see, compensated for the lost selling time.

Here is some background. I work for a corporation that makes surgical instrumentation and supplies. We have seven different product lines, and the products are high quality, with prices that are on the high end yet are reasonable. The competition in the market is fierce, and managed care has caused severe price reduction pressure as well. Overall growth in the market is nonexistent.

I have approximately fifty customers who purchase products routinely from me and several others who order occasionally. On average, each customer orders about five product lines, which yields over 250 targets for many hungry competitors.

Here is how the numbers looked for the year 2000:

Tim Smith 2000 Revenue Growth

New business with current customers	31.2%
+ Price change	3.1
+ New business with new customers	19.3
- Lost customers	0
Revenue growth	53.6%

These growth numbers helped propel me to an all-time corporation record for total revenue in one year. I was given the award for the top sales representative in a corporation with more than twenty-four hundred reps. As of this writing, I have not lost a single product from a customer to a competitor in over five years and counting.

THE MAGIC FORMULA

7 - 0 = 1

You were taught a long time ago that 7 - 0 = 7. So since when does 7 - 0 = 1?

It is hard to look at the same equation that you have seen for years and visualize a different solution. But that is precisely what it takes to become the number one sales representative.

Loyalty-Based Selling energizes you with a new formula to achieve this ultimate goal:

7 Magic Steps - 0 lost customers = #1 sales rep

7 Magic Steps

Why call them Magic Steps? Two reasons.

First, the Magic Steps indeed work like magic. A phenomenal result is achieved, yet the answer is simple and right in front of your eyes. The only way to see the solution is to look at it from a different angle.

Second, visualize a set of seven steps. Once you step on the first one, it begins to escalate upward. As you step on the second, it ascends faster. The speed increases exponentially with each new step, and when you reach the seventh step, you will be at a height you never imagined possible. You will be at the top of the sales world, with all eyes looking up at you.

0 Lost Customers

Why is customer loyalty so valuable? Like many other valuable things, it is rare.

A recent *Wall Street Journal* article stated that customer-to-vendor loyalty is at a twenty-five-year low. Frederick Reichheld, author of *The Loyalty Effect*, revealed that the average U.S. corporation loses half of its customers within five years. Many do so in about three years.

Imagine losing half of your customers in three to five years. That probably makes your stomach churn. Mine too.

The biggest myth in sales is that the best way to increase sales is to focus first on gaining new customers. In fact, statistics show that energy invested in retaining customers yields five times better returns than energy invested in gaining new customers.

Historically, sales reps have focused primarily on gaining new customers. Unfortunately, they lose current customers in the meantime. Dollars go out the back door as fast as or faster than they come in the front.

Reps spend months or even years to acquire a single new customer. It takes seconds to lose one. Sales reps waste considerable time trying to fend off competitive threats as well as attempting to win back lost customers. They lower price and make other costly concessions attempting to do so. This is the harsh reality of focusing first on new customers rather than current ones.

In the Loyalty-Based Selling approach, you will secure the back door before you open the front by focusing first on your current customers and then on new ones. Strong customer satisfaction and relationships will lead to customer loyalty and retention.

Any new business gained will be net growth instead of balancing lost revenue. By solidifying the business with your current customers, there will be fewer competitive attacks. Your relationships with your customers will be so strong that your competitors won't get a foot in the door with them.

You will productively use the time you save from defending or trying to regain current customers to gain new customers. Paradoxically, you will find that you have even more time to gather new customers than you did with the old approach. This makes selling a lot more fun.

Pricing is another reward of the magic formula. You won't have to cut your prices to match your competitors'. While the average rep resorts to price cuts to keep the business, you will be able to earn fair price increases through great service and relationships.

Customers love you and what you offer them. They may even ask you if there is anything else they can buy from you! Just consider how much easier this sale is compared to the one where you beg a prospective customer to look at your product.

Focusing first on current customer loyalty yields an additional dividend: referrals. Sales guru Brian Tracy tells us that nearly 85 percent of all sales come from referrals. It is unlikely that these referrals are coming from customers who are deserted by their sales reps in search of the next sale.

Referrals make the sales process easier and faster. Trust is integral in the relationship between sales rep and customer. In a cold call, trust is at a zero level at best. In fact, trust is usually in the negative numbers. Many customers assume that reps are dishonest until proven otherwise.

But with a referral, some trust has already been established. Your current customer trusts you and your products. The prospective customer trusts the current customer based on their friendship or business relationship. Thus, the trust connection has been made. This catapults the sales process several steps past a cold call starting point.

In sum, keeping customers benefits you in four ways:

1. Retaining the base revenue you have already earned with your current customers
2. Adding new business with current customers
3. Improving pricing
4. Acquiring new customers through customer referrals and through the additional time you will accumulate from this approach

Sales reps often relate best to numbers, so look at this table:

Revenue Growth

	Brian Tierney	Hugh Luvem	Drew Leavem
New business with current customers	22%	9%	3%
+ Price change	4	-6	-10
+ New business with new customers	20	13	8
- Lost customers	0	-16	-30
Total revenue growth	46%	0%	-29%

This table is similar to the one in the previous chapter, which described my personal performance in the year that I wrote this book. The numbers here come from three sales reps employed by a Fortune 100 company. Brian was the number one rep the year he produced these fabulous numbers. He religiously followed the $7 - 0 = 1$ formula and still does. Hugh was middle of the pack, and Drew brought up the rear. (Drew's and Hugh's names have been changed to protect the guilty— guilty of not focusing on current customers first).

Despite the fact that Hugh and Drew gave first priority to new business with new customers, Brian still outperformed them in this category.

Rather than waste time trying to defend his current business, he applied this time to get new customers. Acquiring them was easier due to the bountiful referrals from happy customers. Hugh and Drew spent so much time here that they had decent growth, yet the losses in the other categories negatively offset this percentage.

Lost customers, the last category, provided the biggest gap between the two sales strategies. Brian prided himself on keeping all of his current customers. But Hugh and Drew had no idea how much business was going out the back door because they were focusing narrowly on new customers. Their numbers could have been worse. Statistics show that the average annual loss of customers is 10 to 30 percent. If this is average, obviously some are losing even more.

The total revenue growth category shows the net results. Brian was number one. His growth was 75 percent better than Drew's. Hugh often said, "It feels as if I'm spinning my wheels and gaining no ground." He was right. Without a doubt, the $7 - 0 = 1$ formula works more effectively than the Luvem and Leavem approach.

Most people don't have a clue why this performance difference exists. You now do. The biggest myth in sales has been dispelled.

Shortly you will learn how to make these results a reality.

#1 Sales Rep

The question is "Number One Sales Rep in the _____?" You get to fill in the blank: region, division, company, industry, or world? The only limitations here are self-imposed.

The rewards that accompany this number one status are many. Most companies lavish their top sales rep with recognition. What an awesome feeling it is to give the acceptance speech at the awards banquet with the spotlight and all eyes in the room on you. Being recognized as the champion by your peers and leaders is an experience unparalleled by any other. You will appreciate the trips, plaques, awards, and other gifts that often accompany being number one. The trips sometimes include your spouse or significant other. This provides you with major points that could come in handy in getting you out of the proverbial doghouse later.

Your customers will give you praise and tell you, "You are the reason we do business with your company" or "You give us the best service we have ever received!" There exists no more prestigious or valued source of positive feedback than your customers.

Oh yeah, I almost forgot: the money. Earning the number one award comes with strong dollar earnings. Although reps vary in terms of how much they are motivated by money, all graciously accept it. You will assuredly find a home for it.

Please remember your competitors. Being the number one sales rep means that you kicked more competitive butt than anybody else. That is a lofty and admirable distinction.

I have saved the best for last. Perhaps the greatest reward is knowing in your heart that you are number one. You are the best. That feeling permeates to your soul. It is an accomplishment that no one can ever take away.

Becoming the top sales rep is the burning desire in the hearts of countless reps. The general public is largely unaware that this heated competition exists at virtually every good company that has a sales force of two or more. You know it. You feel it. You live it.

You will be number one!

MAGIC STEP 1

GET THE ANSWERS TO THE TEST

Remember back to high school or college when you were starting to study at 8:00 P.M. the night before the test. Do you recall that feeling in the pit of your stomach at about 7:59 P.M. as you thought about the daunting task that lay ahead? At the moment when that feeling was most acute, if you could have magically (and legally) made the answers to the test appear before your eyes, would you have done it? In a heartbeat.

That would have been awesome! No sleepless night or cold sweats. No Mountain Dew, Jolt, or other artificial sleep inhibitor. No "eenie-meenie-minie-mo" to determine the multiple-choice answers. Instead, you would have casually and confidently strolled into the classroom and aced the test.

All sales reps have that magic at their fingertips. But most don't use it because they are unaware they have it.

How do you use Magic Step 1? Ask your customer the all-important question: "What will it take to provide you with the best service you have ever received?" Voilà! You have the answers to the test!

This step is so simple and the results so profound, yet it is rarely used. In all of your business transactions as a customer, has any sales rep ever asked you that question? Looking at it from a different angle, how many of you have not asked a single one of your key customers this question? Raise your hand. Don't be bashful. You have lots of company.

For those of you who didn't raise your hand, I have one more question. Did you directly ask your customers, or did you infer what their answers would be based on your intimate knowledge of them? Raise your hands again. That's more like it.

With the best intentions, you diligently try to provide excellent service for your customers based on what you think they want. You may believe you are on target, but undoubtedly sometimes you are not. You may be going 100 miles per hour for your customers—but down the wrong street. Don't despair. Magic Step 1 enables you to get the answers to the test before you take it. The approach is called Best Service Ever...Guaranteed. Initiate this the first time you meet your customer. Consider this sample dialogue:

> *Robert:* Hi, Mary. Thank you very much for meeting with me today.
> *Mary:* Thank you, Robert, for coming out here to see me.
> *Robert:* Mary, before we begin our discussion about the product we spoke of on the phone, may I ask you a very important question?
> *Mary:* Sure, Robert. What's the question?
> *Robert:* I realize that I am starting from scratch, and it will take considerable effort to achieve the following. Mary, it is my goal to provide you with the best service you have ever received. Your satisfaction is my top priority. People have different preferences. Could you please share with me exactly what it will take to provide you with the best service you have ever received?

Mary: You know, I have never been asked that question before. Robert, I am impressed that you care enough to ask what is important to me. This is what it will take to provide me with the best service I have ever received....

You may have mixed emotions at this point. On one hand, you may be excited to implement Magic Step 1 with your new customers. On the other hand, you may sigh and think, "That's great for new customers, but what about customers with whom I have worked for years? It's too late to use this step with them."

Good news! It is never too late to initiate the Best Service Ever...Guaranteed plan with your current customers. It is equally important to ask them the same question, though in a slightly different way:

Robert: You know, Mary, I have never really asked you the following question, and I should have when we first met. I think I have a good idea what your answer might be, but I will never know for sure unless I ask. Mary, it is my goal to provide you with the best service you have ever received. Your satisfaction is my top priority. People have different preferences. Could you please share with me exactly what it will take to provide you with the best service you have ever received?

It is not critical to use the exact words from these sample dialogues (certainly many of your customers are not named Mary), but it is key to maintain the substance. Even more important, you must practice, practice, and practice. This is an invaluable question, and you want to treat it accordingly.

What have you accomplished by asking this one question? A lot.

For starters, you now have the answers to the test. You know exactly what you need to do to give your customers the best service they have ever received. You will gain your customer's highest level of satisfaction. You will ace this test! In fact, this is guaranteed. Magic Step 7 is patiently waiting for you at the end of this book. This step serves as the seal to the guarantee.

It is far from guaranteed for most corporations. They spend millions of dollars researching what it will take to get customer satisfaction. They laboriously investigate what service levels their customers need. They send out customer survey after customer survey. They invest countless hours interpreting the results. But once they have the results, most haven't a clue as to what to do with them. The good ones actually implement new programs geared to improve service and customer satisfaction.

Do these programs work? For some customers they do, and for others they don't. Why? Because every customer is different. Each has unique preferences and a unique definition of what "the best service ever" means. The programs may make sense for the group as a "whole," but the "hole" in that logic is clear.

There is one other minor detail: when corporations ask the question, it is typically after they have worked with the customer for a period of time.

You, on the other hand, get to ask your customers the question *before* you have started doing business with them. You have the opportunity to treat your customers as they wish from the start.

The answers you receive from the Best Service Ever...Guaranteed question might surprise you. To be sure, there will be some common requests such as honesty and fast response time. However, you will likely hear some things you couldn't have guessed.

When I asked my customer Kim Schooley this question, she asked me to refrain from wearing cologne when visiting her. She has a serious allergy to certain perfumes and colognes, which causes her to break out in hives. No problem. I leave the Old Spice and Hi Karate on the shelf the days that I visit her.

Susan Waisanen informed me that she once received a birthday card from a rep and felt that was especially thoughtful. I send her cards for her birthday, Christmas, Valentine's Day, St. Patrick's Day, Arbor Day, Flag Day....

John Libert voiced a preference for scheduling appointments with sales reps on Thursdays. I always offer to meet with him on Thursdays.

None of these actions has been difficult to perform. All of them would have been nearly impossible to guess.

So by asking just one question, you can save your company millions of research dollars.

In addition, this question unleashes the power of the ever-famous self-fulfilling prophecy: If people expect something to happen, invariably it happens—or, more accurately, they perceive that it happens.

You have clearly stated your intentions. Your customers are poised and ready for the best service ever. They expect to receive it. You simply execute the plan that they so kindly have given you, and you are golden.

You have clearly differentiated yourself from your competition. In this era, products from one company to the next are often similar, so differentiation in other areas is the deciding factor in a buying decision. You have just taken a huge first step ahead of your competition. And all that from one little question. How did it work? Like magic!

You are now standing on Magic Step 1. The steps have started to ascend. Enjoy the ride!

The magic continues. Your sales numbers grow...
You now have the answers you need to know.

MAGIC STEP 2
MAKE FRIENDS

Sales has evolved considerably. In the initial phase, the Adversarial Era, the approach was for sales reps to sell their products to customers whether they needed them or not. The best salespeople were the ones who could trick customers into buying products they really didn't need. Sayings such as "Selling ice to an Eskimo" come to mind.

Then (thankfully) a gradual transition began to take place to the Needs/Features/Benefits Era. Now selling was based on determining customers' needs and explaining the features and benefits of the products that could meet them. Customers began to receive fairness and honesty. Still, there was a heavy emphasis on closing. Reps were taught forty-two ways to close the sale, and certainly not all of them were in the customers' best interests.

The most recent advance has brought the Partnership Era. Establishing win-win relationships with mutual goals is the foundation for this strategy. The focus is on providing solutions rather than features and benefits. Emphasis on closing has given way to sharing ideas, innovations, and resources. This approach, which I fully endorse, has yielded excellent results.

Should you stop here, satisfied that this is the best you can do? I think that is a great idea—for your competitors. For you, partnership selling is a stepping-stone on the way to far greater heights: friendship.

Why Friendship?

The word *partnership* itself sounds a bit formal. It gives the impression of a purely business arrangement. Although partnerships effectively create strong business relationships, they don't address personal relationships.

Has anyone ever heard a statement like this one: "You will never get the business from that customer. The Acme rep is a good friend of the key decision maker!"

You hate to hear that about your competition. You know how tough it will be to get the business from that customer. You may feel that it is not even worth trying.

That is exactly how you want your competitors to feel. Your goal is to make good friends with your customers. Friends make loyal customers, who are not attracted by competitive promotions and do not leave you at the first sign of difficulty. Friends are understanding and tolerant of your mistakes; they stick with you through challenging times and work with you to create the great times too; they refer you to their friends. The value of having customers as friends is immeasurable. It is important, of course, to develop *sincere* friendships, not just convenient ones. Pretending to be friends with customers, using them to close sales, and disposing of them thereafter is a tactic that will come back to haunt you, and rightfully so.

There is a bonus to this approach of turning customers into friends: You gain friends. Many of my customers who have become my friends have made job changes and are no longer my customers, but a number of them are still my good friends.

Friendship goes beyond building rapport, which is surface level and short-term in nature. True friendships are genuine, deep, and long lasting. A strong friendship is the pinnacle of all relationships. It is the most loyal bond possible between two people and is the glue that keeps couples happily married for the long term. (Those of you with young kids and busy lives know that marriage longevity is certainly not due to frequent love-making.) Why shouldn't you pursue the strongest and most loyal bond you can with your customers?

The plan is to treat your customers as *personal* friends who happen to have *business* needs. Now look at the situation from a slightly different angle, and the solution is clearly visible.

Establish Trust—Immediately

Trust is a good place to start because it is essential to successful selling. Customers don't buy from people they can't trust.

Trust is also critical to a sound friendship. A friend is not a friend if you cannot trust him. Many customers naturally distrust sales reps, who may have deceived them in the past. The earlier you can overcome this predisposition, the better. Only then can your friendship begin. How do you do this? Tell them. Then show them.

Again, use the power of the self-fulfilling prophecy to your advantage. Let's pick up where you left off with Magic Step 1.

Robert has just heard Mary, his prospective customer, tell him how to provide her with the best service that she has ever received based on her unique preferences. Now it is his turn to inform his customer about his unique style:

> *Robert:* Thank you, Mary, for sharing your unique thoughts with me about providing you with the best service you have ever received. In turn, I would like to share with you a bit about my style as a rep. First, I am flexible. I will happily customize my approach to meet the specific requests that you have just given me. Second, I am a person you can trust. I may not be the most suave sales rep you have met, but you will find no one more honest and trustworthy.

With this approach, you reverse customer expectations. Your customers transpose subconscious negative expectations on trust into conscious positive expectations. You have set the self-fulfilling prophecy in motion. Keep in mind that trust is an incremental process, not an instantaneous one. You earn trust a little at a time.

You have now completed the first half of that really complicated formula: Tell them, then show them. Even after you tell your customers that you are trustworthy, some will still doubt you, so it's important that you follow through with the second half and show them.

It is very simple: *Always be honest.* It takes only one little white lie to destroy trust. Trust is like an expensive vase. Once you have broken it, it will never be the same again. No matter how diligently you try to glue the vase back together, the cracks can still be seen. The cracks can always be seen with broken trust as well. One fabrication can erase thousands of honest interactions.

Besides, it takes too much work to try to keep track of the stories. You never have to keep track of the truth. This reminds me of when I first started in sales.

I lived in Southern California. It was my first day of my first sales job, and I was clueless. I had an 8:00 A.M. meeting in Los Angeles with Joe McCarthy, the key decision maker at one of my largest accounts. The meeting started promptly, and to my surprise, it went exceptionally well.

We really hit it off. We discussed our backgrounds and found that we had a lot in common. Even better, our product solutions fit his business needs like a glove. The meeting continued in a positive direction until I looked at my watch. It was 9:05 A.M., and my next appointment was in Irvine at 9:30 A.M. If you know Southern California, you are already laughing. I did not have a prayer of making it on time.

Nevertheless, I quickly concluded the meeting with plans to follow up with Joe the following week. I jumped in the car and drove as fast as I could go, which was about 15 miles per hour in the good stretches due to traffic. My car phone was to be installed the next week, so I could not easily call ahead.

As my knuckles grew whiter, I began to concoct reasons to give my customer for my tardiness. *I was held at gunpoint.* That was fitting for L.A. but a little too creative. *I had a flat tire.* That one wasn't creative enough. *The traffic was terrible.* Duh, this is Los Angeles. I decided to settle for the truth.

I was more than a little late when I walked into Caryn Brown's office, a key decision maker at another one of my largest accounts (for the moment). I tried to disguise that look of panic, but the beads of sweat on my forehead gave me away. I sincerely apologized for being late. I informed Caryn that my previous meeting had gone so well that I lost track of time. I asked for her pardon.

Caryn was well aware that I was new, and she was quite sympathetic. (As I write this, it strikes me that the word *sympathetic* is a combination of *sympathy* [her] and *pathetic* [me]. How appropriate!) She informed me that she understood.

Then she said, "Besides, I spoke with my husband shortly after you met with him, and he told me that you might be a little late. Did you know that I am married to Joe McCarthy?"

My heart stopped beating, probably because it was lodged in my throat. My first day on the job had almost been my last. I had come close to losing any chance of trust with two of my largest customers.

That experience embedded a permanent lesson in me: to tell the truth—always.

Take It Personal

Take your relationships to a personal level as soon as your customers are ready. For most customers, that is immediately.

One effective way to accomplish this in your very first meeting with a customer is to share information about your background in exchange for background information from her. It is critical that you initiate this conversation with an explanation of intent: to work together with a person, not just a job title. Let's go back to our example:

Robert: Mary, since we have just met, it might be helpful if we exchange a little information about our backgrounds. We will be able to relate better to each other beyond our job titles.

Start by reviewing topics about yourself: hometown, high school, college, previous work experience, spouse, kids, hobbies. This should be brief—no more than two minutes. You could go on forever about these topics, but you respect their time.

Your customers will reciprocate. Customers vary in how much information they feel comfortable sharing in a first meeting. Interestingly, they often feel quite comfortable with this conversation.

To get a head start, you may be able to learn something about a certain customer prior to your first call. The following are just some of the sources that can be helpful in this pursuit:

- Reps from other companies who currently call on the customer
- People with your current company who worked with the customer previously and now are in a different position
- Other customers who may know this customer
- The customer's secretary
- Newspaper articles
- The Internet

By learning about a customer in advance, you can better target your conversation for this particular person.

Is this a waste of time? No. This is an excellent investment of time with a considerable return. You have already taken your relationship to a personal level:

- You have opened the door to find something in common with your customers. The topics you just discussed are especially fertile ground. Good friends must have something in common.
- You have given your customers the opportunity to talk about something other than work. That can be refreshing. Most

parents love to talk about their families. Interests and hobbies are great topics too.

- You have shown your customers that you care about them as persons, not only as businesspeople.

- You have just taken the first big step toward having your customers view you as a person rather than the evil stereotype of a deceitful sales rep. They must see you as a person before they trust you as a friend.

The tone of these initial meetings differs from the purely business meetings your competitors have. You may have more personal relationships with your customers in one meeting than your competitors have after years of meetings. You have clearly differentiated yourself from your competitors—again! Will you be able to accomplish this in every initial meeting? No. Some situations and personality styles are unsuited for this exchange in a first meeting. The point is to do it as soon as the customer is ready.

Once you have initiated personal relationships with your customers, it is easy to build on them. In future meetings, pick up where you left off.

Friendly Facts

How do you keep track of all this information you gather? You may have hundreds of customers you work with. And sometimes it's months between meetings with a person. How do you remember kids' names and hobbies? (With the fast pace of my job, I am lucky to remember my own name by the end of the day.)

It becomes much easier to remember these important facts as your friendship grows with a person. At the beginning of a new friendship, though, it can be challenging. You may use an aid to help you with your recall. I call it a Friendly Facts sheet. Here it is filled out for Robert's customer Mary. Notice that only some of the categories are filled in as a result of their first meeting.

Friendly Facts

NAME *Mary Meagher*_____PREVIOUS EXPERIENCE_____

INTERESTS ___ *Chicago Bears football, golf, jogging* _____

_____

SPOUSE NAME/BIRTHDAYS/INTERESTS _____

_____

KIDS' NAMES/BIRTHDAYS/INTERESTS_____

    Richie, 1987 _____

    Grace, 1989 _____

_____

_____

HIGH SCHOOL/YR. _____UNDERGRAD/YR. *Northwestern* _____

GRAD/YR. _____

HOMETOWN *Palatine, IL*____SENSITIVE SUBJECTS_____

RELIGION _____BIRTHDAY_____GIFT IDEAS_____

Let's say that Robert has his second meeting with Mary a month after the first. In the meantime, he has taken a trip to Hawaii, which he won in a company contest, and he feels as if he left a portion of his memory on the beach next to the empty piña colada glasses. Upon his return, he does not recall all of the specifics of his personal discussion with Mary. He knows she has two children but can't recall their names, so he reviewed his Friendly Facts sheet before the meeting. The conversation when they meet goes as follows:

Robert: Hi, Mary. It is nice to see you again.

Mary: Nice to see you too, Robert.

Robert: Did you watch the Chicago Bears game this past weekend?

Mary: I sure did. Weren't the Bears awesome?!

Robert: Absolutely! Did Richie and Grace watch the game with you?

Mary: Oh, yes. Both my kids and my husband, Tom, are avid Chicago fans. By the way, Robert, you mentioned your daughter had a birthday party coming up. How did that go?

Doesn't that beat the "What nice weather we are having" as an opener? You can easily pick up where you left off without feeling the discomfort of forgetting something you should have remembered. As you gather additional information, you add it to the Friendly Facts sheet. In this case, Robert jotted down Tom's name after the meeting.

I need to make a crucial clarification here. This is a memory aid, not a survey. Gather information gradually over time, not all at once. The goal is not to fill in all the blanks to get the task done because your company requires you to. It is truly for your own benefit. The intent is to use the Friendly Facts sheet as a reference to support your memory. As your friendships grow with your customers, you may find yourself no longer referring to the sheet.

Notice how concise this tool is. Due to its brevity, it is likely that you will use it routinely.

I have included a blank Friendly Facts sheet on the following page for your use. This format allows you to gather information on multiple contacts per page to conserve space in your files.

For those of you who bring portable computers on each call, you may create a similar sheet on your computer. By all means, amend the sheet to your personal preference and needs.

Tour the House

What do you typically do when you visit a friend's home for the first time? You are given a tour of the house.

Your friend first introduces her husband and three children to you. She explains what activities each child is involved in. You ask the kids questions about these important topics, and they enjoy telling you about all the fun they are having. Her husband then describes what he does for

Friendly Facts

NAME_____PREVIOUS EXPERIENCE_____

INTERESTS _____

_____

SPOUSE NAME/BIRTHDAYS/INTERESTS _____

_____

KIDS' NAMES/BIRTHDAYS/INTERESTS_____

_____

_____

_____

_____

HIGH SCHOOL/YR. _____UNDERGRAD/YR. _____

GRAD/YR. _____

HOMETOWN _____SENSITIVE SUBJECTS_____

RELIGION _____BIRTHDAY_____GIFT IDEAS_____

NAME_____PREVIOUS EXPERIENCE_____

INTERESTS _____

_____

SPOUSE NAME/BIRTHDAYS/INTERESTS _____

_____

KIDS' NAMES/BIRTHDAYS/INTERESTS_____

_____

_____

_____

_____

HIGH SCHOOL/YR. _____UNDERGRAD/YR. _____

GRAD/YR. _____

HOMETOWN _____SENSITIVE SUBJECTS_____

RELIGION _____BIRTHDAY_____GIFT IDEAS_____

a living. You ask him questions about his profession, and he gladly explains to you the finer points of his work.

As you converse with her family, you have the opportunity to see how they interact together. You observe how they treat each other. There is some bickering between two of the kids, a sign that they are breathing (bickering and breathing go hand in hand for siblings). Overall, they get along quite well as a family.

The tour begins. Your friend explains the thought process involved in the decoration of each room. You ask many questions to learn more about how she created such a beautiful home. You praise her as you move from room to room.

The kitchen is immaculately clean and organized. You walk through the family room, where the family spends time together. This room also serves as a shrine for trophies and awards. You learn who won them and for what activities. You compliment them accordingly. Your friend finishes the main level with a visit to the living and dining rooms. The family entertains here.

Up the stairs you go. You learn who lives in each bedroom. You observe the personal decoration in each room. One is adorned with sports pennants and posters. In the words of my mother, it is a pigsty. The next looks like the Hard Rock Cafe, neatly decorated with a musical motif. A third room is for the baby and is a tribute to Winnie the Pooh. The master bedroom has a contemporary decor. A quick stop in the master bath gives you insight into . . . her husband's favorite books.

The tour ends with a quick trip down to the basement level. You see the kids' playroom. Even that is clean and well organized. A quick peek in the back room reveals the foundation of the home, the furnace, and the hot water heater.

Your friend informs you that they need a new hot water heater. You ask her a few questions to determine specifically what is wrong with it. She tells you that it just doesn't produce enough hot water to meet the family's needs. You ask further what impact that has had on the family. She illustrates the ramifications of the problem with a story about how the kids were late for school yesterday because their showers were delayed, and she and her husband were late for work too. You empathize with her.

How is all this relevant? I bet you see the analogy. What an awesome sales call this would be if it took place in your customer's "house" (business) with her "family" (co-workers). Taking a "tour of the house" offers huge benefits to your friendship-building strategy.

The approach is easy. Ask your customers if they will give you a tour of the company. You may even choose to use the phrase "tour of the house" to set an informal, relaxed tone. The vast majority will oblige. They take pride in their company and enjoy showing it off.

Meet as many people as you can. If you meet them in their offices, observe the decorations. An office, like a bedroom, offers insight into people and what's important in their lives. Notice the awards, photographs, books, posters, neatness, and organization. Learn what you can about their personal and business lives. In essence, initiate a friendship with each person you meet. Your goal is to make friends with everyone in the building.

A story my good friend John Nicko once told me is relevant here. John was a sales rep for Rolm with responsibility for telephone system hardware. He had received a lead about a sizable company interested in purchasing a new phone system and called the company to follow up. He was greeted rather rudely by Elaine, the phone receptionist. Although he wanted to remind her in no uncertain terms that her company had asked for his help through the lead, he remained courteous and polite. Answering with warmth and patience every question she asked was painful but necessary. Elaine, the guard dog receptionist, eventually let him advance to the person who sent him the lead.

As the sales process progressed, Elaine began to warm up to John. He wisely asked for her input and learned what was important to her in a phone system. He also began a relationship on a personal level.

John learned some bad news in speaking with Elaine: The other company in contention for the business was an industry giant with better name recognition and more resources: AT&T. He thought he was dead in the water. But as it turned out, John won the business. AT&T had a better name in the industry, but Rolm had a better sales rep.

Connor, the rep for AT&T, took a different approach with Elaine. In his eyes, she was an unpleasant obstacle, and he retaliated with the same rudeness that he received from Elaine. He avoided her when possible because she slowed him down with her inane questions. She was just a measly receptionist who was a pain in the butt. Unfortunately for Connor, that pain in the butt was the owner's wife.

The importance of making friends with everyone in the company cannot be overemphasized.

Companies and families share similar dynamics. It is important to learn the role that each person plays in the company. Observe how they interact with each other. If there is tension between two people, note this as well.

Observe firsthand how the operations function. Through questions and observation, learn the specifics of how processes flow. You may uncover needs that you never would have thought of if you had not taken the tour. Would you have thought to ask your friend about her furnace problem if you hadn't taken the tour?

Investing valuable time in an informal, conversational setting infuses the personal element into your interaction. Your praise and compliments make your friend feel better than ever before. Your sincere interest in your friend, your friend's associates, and your friend's company strengthen your friendship.

Use this approach over as many calls as needed. If you have not met a key person, ask your tour guide to introduce you the next time. The same is true for observing certain work processes. You can always ask to visit that spot on the tour at a later date.

Your friendships are growing by the minute. And so is your customer loyalty.

Ask, Listen, and Observe

Entire books are dedicated to the topic of how to ask questions in a sales call. Plenty of material exists on listening skills too. This section is not designed to replace that information. Rather, the intent is to shed new light on a few key principles that are often lost in the mountains of detail.

The objective is to get to know your friends better. You need to understand your friends' motivations, goals, and priorities. You must learn what is important to them, how they are measured, and how you can help them excel in their jobs and their lives overall. Friends help friends.

Ask

It is essential to ask questions in the sales process. It is equally important not to sound like a typical sales rep when you do it.

Keep in mind you are visiting with a friend as if you are in her house. Wouldn't it be just a little awkward if during this visit you hauled out a list of rehearsed questions and started firing away? Or if you used that typical "sales rep" tone that you have heard on the videotapes during your sales training? Or if you took notes on every single word your friend said?

Leave that canned style of questioning to your competitors. Ask questions of your customer friends in the same fashion that you ask questions of your noncustomer friends.

Take notes only when appropriate during the call. Taking notes on detailed items that you wouldn't be expected to remember shows interest and organizational skills. Copying every word out of the customer's mouth changes the tone of the visit to that of a survey. Take copious notes immediately *after* the call.

This isn't to say that you're unprepared. On the contrary, you're even better prepared than your competitors are. You know exactly what topics to cover and what objectives you intend to accomplish in advance of the sales call. The more comfortable you feel with the information before the call, the more relaxed you feel during the call. In turn, your customers feel more relaxed.

To ensure that you have loyal customers, you must know that your products or services will meet their needs. As you increase your knowledge of your products and your customers, the tendency to make assumptions multiplies. Assuming that you know your customers' needs can be fatal. Each person has unique needs, which can change over time. By asking questions, you may get answers that surprise you. You learn only when you ask, not when you tell.

Many of your competitors ask questions about needs. What can you do differently?

Typically competitors ask only about the business. But you are interested in both what the business and personal ramifications are of these needs.

Inquire about the business implications first. What will happen if these needs go unfulfilled? What will be the results? How will that affect the business goals and objectives? Remember from the analogy the problem your friend had with the hot water heater capacity and the ramifications of her kids being late for school as a result. Asking these questions shows you care about the success of the business.

Follow by asking about the impact of these needs on a personal level:

"How will this affect you?"

"How do you feel about it?"

"How will this influence your personal goals and objectives?"

"Who else will this affect? How so? And how will this influence their personal goals and objectives?"

Asking these questions shows you care about the success and feelings of your friends. By taking action on them, you will endear your customers to you permanently.

Listen

Think about your best friends for a moment. Are they good listeners? Do they care about you, your interests, and your lives? Absolutely. If they do not, they aren't truly good friends.

Listening is even more important than asking. If you don't listen to the answer, what good is it to ask the question?

Most reps are better talkers than listeners. Sometimes even when they think they are listening well, they are not. They are so focused on asking good questions that they start thinking ahead to the next question in the middle of their customer's response to the first one, so they don't actually listen to their customer's complete answer. They miss valuable information after they stop actively listening. Has this ever happened to you? Me too.

Think about the last time you traveled with your manager. After the sales call, you discussed how it went. You learned that she heard a few things that you didn't. She had an advantage: She wasn't thinking about the next question.

If it takes a moment after the response to think of your next question, that's all right. Brief silence may feel a little awkward at first, but it won't hurt you. Your customers appreciate that you have listened so attentively.

It is important to show your customer both verbally and nonverbally that you are actively listening. The best way to do this verbally is to intersperse a few words of acknowledgment during the course of conversation. There is one magic phrase better than all the rest put together: "I understand." That feels good to the customer, who feels understood, accepted, justified, and even profound.

It feels much better than, "I know" or "Right," where the focus is on you, not the customer. These phrases reduce the value of what the customer is saying. It implies that you already know this, that you are unimpressed.

Other good acknowledgments include: "Great," "Yes," "Oh really," and "Fantastic!" A lot of value is packed into these few words.

Nonverbally, you can virtually carry on a conversation with your facial expressions. A smile, a raised eyebrow, a frown, a knit brow: All of these communicate something different. Use these nonverbals in an unobtrusive way to stay connected. There is no interruption or distraction with any sound, yet the customer knows that you understand her.

You show respect when you listen sincerely to your customers, and you therefore make your customers feel valued and important. The focus is on your friends, not on you. It is good for the ego to be understood.

Speaking of ego, that is another reason that many reps talk too much: They feel good when they are on stage and want to dazzle customers with their knowledge and intellect. You must resist this temptation. Making customers feel great about themselves is the best way to pump up your own ego.

People often say, "I am looking forward to talking to you." From this statement, it is clear that society places a greater emphasis on talking rather than listening. Perhaps you should say, "I am looking forward to listening to you." Maybe that is a little too corny, but at the very least, you should say, "I am looking forward to speaking *with* you."

There is a saying, "You have two ears and one mouth. You should use them in that proportion." I endorse that recommendation and suggest you take it a step further. A three-to-one ratio would be even better. By striving to listen three times as much as you talk, you are assuredly on the path to successful listening. This may sound more challenging than it really is. In fact, this ratio happens quite naturally by asking good questions and listening completely to the answers. First ask, then listen. Then...

Observe

Clearly the most underrated of the three, observation is something you don't read much about. Nevertheless, you can gain valuable insight by observing the person, place, and people interactions.

When you observe the person you are speaking with, look for body language. Note posture, hand gestures, eye contact, and facial expression. Pay attention to speech. Tone, pace, volume, and inflection are key factors.

There are whole books written on this topic that describe the potential meaning of these different elements. Here, let's focus on two axioms you can put to use immediately that cover all body language and speech factors:

1. *Mirror the person you are speaking with.* Your customer's comfort level increases with the similarity of your body language and speech. For example, if one person is speaking ten words per second while the other is speaking at a rate of ten seconds per word, both might experience frustration. The responsibility is yours to adapt your style to that of your customer.

2. *Observe any changes in your customer's body language and speech during your meeting.* More important, take appropriate action once you notice a change. For instance, if during a sales call, your customer suddenly folds her arms and sits back in her chair, heed this red flag. Your action depends on the circumstances. If you are uncertain of the reason for this change in posture, you might simply ask your customer if she has a concern. This might uncover an objection or unlock a gold mine of valuable information. Or if you know that you have touched on a particularly sensitive topic, you might change the subject. The key is to take some action to alleviate your customer's defensiveness and discomfort.

Ask. Listen. Observe. It works.

The Forgotten Compliment

Why don't people receive compliments very frequently anymore? You need to look no further than the mirror for a share of the responsibility.

Based on the nature of sales, there is significant focus on performance. Graphs, computer reports, annual merit reviews, and ranking sheets abound. You are inundated with numbers and measurements: percentage of quota, percentage growth, growth dollars, percentage of expense budget, and others. Management reminds you constantly of your status in each of these areas, so it is no surprise that you approach a customer with a "me" focus. As you walk in to see your customer, you are calculating the impact the sale will have on your numbers. You may be so busy thinking of your numbers that complimenting your customer takes a back seat.

Another reason you might not praise your customers as often as you should is that you assume that they don't need it. This is especially true of very competent, high-level people. Most figure these people already know they are great. They must hear it ten times a day.

Quite the contrary. High-level people may hear compliments less and need them more than the rest. If everyone assumes that everyone else is complimenting these successful people, ultimately nobody gives them praise. Furthermore, many accomplished people thrive on recognition. It is often their primary motivation. Praise fuels their engines.

The workplace itself shares the remainder of the responsibility for why people don't receive compliments frequently. With downsizing, companies are running lean. Businesses can be so focused on the bottom-line results that the people who deliver the results get lost in the shuffle. Numbers, not people, matter.

Management skill is often lacking. Managers spend most of their time telling people what they are doing wrong rather than what they are doing right. Some managers are so overworked that they don't find time to compliment their employees. This does not excuse them, though it does explain why the compliment is often forgotten.

The next question is, Why should you make the effort to compliment your customers? Think back to the last time that you received an unexpected compliment. Did it make your day? Indeed!

Do the same for your customers. Compliment them sincerely, and they feel great about themselves. What a fantastic lift you give them in the midst of today's business culture. The focus is on them, not on their numbers or yours. You fan their fire. You bring smiles to their faces. In turn, your customers feel great about you. It is natural for people to like those who make them feel good about themselves.

It is a reflex action to compliment the person who compliments you. It's as if there has to be an even balance of compliments in a relationship. If one party goes up one, the other has to even the score. You won't be surprised if, after you praise your customer, a compliment about you or your product comes back to you. Reciprocity can be fun.

Most important when you compliment people is that the compliment be sincere. A customer spots an insincere compliment in a blink. It produces the opposite effect of what you are attempting to achieve. As you get in the habit of praising your customers, notice how easy it is to find something praiseworthy in virtually everyone you work with. It is the rare exception that someone has no redeeming qualities. The compliment must be from the heart and appropriate. The following subjects are fair game for compliments:

Work-related performance

Staff performance

Talents

Awards

Efficiency

Quality

The organization

Work environment

Activities away from work

Family accomplishments

One topic requires caution: Compliments on appearance can make some people uncomfortable. It can also be misperceived as a proposition.

The more specific the compliment, the better it is. Complimenting a customer's on-time record has far greater value than saying, "You do nice work here." A specific comment is thoughtful, personal, and meaningful.

Compliments can be verbal or written. An extremely effective method is to send a letter to a customer's manager describing how awesome the customer is and specifically why. Send a copy of the letter to your customer as well. Your friend will love you for it.

Timing plays an important role. The best time to compliment is when someone least expects it. When there is no hint of obligation, the impact is most powerful.

A short story illustrates the value of a well-timed, sincere compliment. Dr. Weber, a prominent neurosurgeon, was trying my new craniotome for the first time on a brain tumor surgery. A craniotome is a special drill used to remove a piece of skull for access to the brain. My role was to observe the surgery and provide any technical support that he or his staff needed in relation to the drill.

The surgery was a success. Dr. Weber removed the tumor completely, and the prognosis for the patient was full recovery. Afterward I spoke with Dr. Weber in the doctors' lounge. This is the customary time for a sales rep to ask a surgeon how he liked the new product. Instead, I turned the spotlight on him: "Dr. Weber, I have the pleasure of working with most of the neurosurgeons in Michigan. Many of them are talented. I can confidently say, however, that I have not witnessed better surgical technique than yours. Your precision and decisiveness are very impressive."

"Thank you very much, Tim," he responded. "I was very pleased with the outcome of the surgery. Your craniotome is excellent. Clearly it cuts more precisely and with greater control than any other on the market. I will recommend the purchase of this new technology immediately. Tim, you are the best rep in the entire world!"

All right, I made the last sentence up. But the rest is accurate. I did indeed feel like the best rep on the planet after hearing his response. Dr. Weber felt great too, I later learned.

Months later, after we became friends, Dr. Weber and I were discussing the topic of praise. We were speaking of the lack of praise in the workplace. He shared these feelings with me: "This may come as a surprise to you, Tim, but I very infrequently receive praise. Maybe people think my ego is such that I don't need it. It is a rare day when someone tells me I did a great job. In fact, I remember distinctly a compliment that you gave me many months ago. You complimented my surgical technique. I pride myself on my precision. That really meant a lot to me."

Wow! Such little effort. Such big impact. He was right: I was surprised, and pleasantly.

This compliment had such a strong impact on Dr. Weber because it was sincere, appropriate, specific, and unexpected. It immediately put me on a higher plateau than my competitors. We were on our way to becoming good friends.

Do you think Dr. Weber's feedback on my drill would have been as positive had I taken the typical self-focused sales rep approach? I'll never know. Perhaps I should ask my competition. Dr. Weber tried their new drill too. They thought theirs was vastly superior to mine. They are still scratching their heads wondering how they lost that one.

All Work and No Play

For a variety of reasons, an increasing percentage of customer interactions are in a business setting. Many sales reps aren't "entertaining" their customers as much as they used to, and they are missing a golden opportunity.

Busy schedules and budget cuts are two principal reasons for this reduction. Schedules have become tight for customers and reps. Many don't even eat lunch, much less make time for a business lunch away from work. A *USA Today* article states that only 12 percent of businesspeople take an hour for lunch now.

Reps are facing increased requests to spend time away from their families. Many already travel overnight as a routine part of their jobs. In addition, companies are scheduling sales meetings over the weekends. Trade shows and conferences also fall on weekends.

Furthermore, sales reps have seen drastic cuts in expense budgets. No longer do they have carte blanche with the company credit card. Tax law changes have substantially decreased the tax write-off value of "entertainment." The lean and mean operating philosophy strikes again.

Is it even worth attempting to address the challenge of spending time with customers outside the work setting? Absolutely.

People sometimes take on a work persona in the business setting; only a fraction of their whole person is visible. But when they are away from work, their guard comes down. This applies to both your customers and you. You can interact real person to real person. Getting past the surface to form a deeper, more personal bond becomes feasible. The work persona shield vanishes.

The work setting is stressful and distracting. Completing a full sentence without a phone call, beeper, or some other interruption is difficult. It is challenging to have any meaningful meetings under these conditions. Besides, interacting away from work is fun, and sharing fun together strengthens friendships. It also beats the heck out of another stressful day at the office.

"This all sounds great, but how do I overcome the time and money obstacles?" you ask. I hear you.

When, who, what, and how. These four questions provide your answers.

When?

After the workday used to be the best time to get together with customers. It still is for many, though for some it has changed because of family activity after work: the tee-ball game for Taylor, dance class for Morgan, a parent-teacher conference for mom and dad—and this is just a slow night. Good luck taking this customer out for some fine dining.

Before the workday begins has become an opportune time to bond with customers. The majority of sales reps are missing this opportunity. Certainly, meeting over breakfast is a viable option. Bonding before work also provides a hidden benefit: The mind is free and clear of the barrage of stresses from a typical day. You enjoy each other while both of you are still fresh.

Who?

By including your families in this time together away from work, the options are endless. Many of the time constraints evaporate. Nights and weekends become fair game. Neither you nor your customers have to spend time away from your families.

You may choose to involve spouses only or include the children as well. Both alternatives yield great benefits. Not only does it become more feasible to get the time together with your customers, it also steers your friendships into another dimension.

A close family is an extension of a person. If you don't know the family, you don't know an important piece of your customer. Forming a relationship with the family enriches your bond with your customer as a complete person.

You have shown your customer that you care about her as a person. You understand how essential her family is to her. Rather than place obstacles in the way, you have facilitated their time together as a family.

Once you are in good graces with the family, the party is over for your competitors. For your customer to dump you and choose to do business with your competitor, he would have to face his wife and kids in addition to facing you. Even if he had the gumption to deliver the bad news to you, it is unlikely he would be able to weather the wrath of the family.

What?

I mentioned the term "entertainment" previously and put the word in quotation marks for a reason: Your competitors use that term. For you, the term is a misnomer. People don't entertain close friends. They entertain acquaintances, business associates, and customers who aren't friends. The connotations are formal and distant.

To attempt to come up with a trendy term instead of "entertainment" would be silly. This is not a trendy approach. It is very basic and effective. You simply want to invest time together with your customers away from work—as friends do.

How?

Can it be expensive? Yes. Can it be inexpensive? For sure.

Many customers are tuned in to the fact that the price of the products they buy must cover the expenses needed to make and market them. Customers know that if expenses increase, so will prices. Spending too lavishly can turn customers off for this very reason. In addition, some customers can feel almost bribed if the expense is exorbitant.

The expense depends on your customer's taste and your budget. It is critical to do something that is fitting for your customer based on your strong knowledge of her. Choose something that you can really enjoy together. Consider the following ideas:

Outdoor Activities (warm weather): Bike, hike, roller-blade, water-ski, jet-ski/waverunner, boat, rock-climb, parachute, fish, hunt

Outdoor Activities (cold weather): Downhill ski, cross-country ski, sled, snowmobile, snowboard

Sporting Event (attend): Major league professional, minor league professional, college, high school

Sporting Event (play): Golf, tennis, racquetball, squash, basketball, volleyball, softball

Still More: Bowling, jogging, health spa, massage/manicure/facial, motivational seminar, amusement park, ice capades, circus, casino, comedy club, boat cruise, outlet mall shopping, art gallery or museum, aquarium, fashion show, hot-air balloon, wine tasting, microbrew tasting, concert, play/opera/ballet

Going solo, with spouse, or with spouse and kids are all options. Mornings, nights, or weekends give you choices as well. The obstacles are cleared from your path. Have fun!

How would you like to be in your competitors' shoes now? Ouch! Are they going to take your business away? Fat chance!

As you progress through the book, remember that every action you take for your customer is an act of kindness for a good friend. If you are uncertain how to proceed in a challenging situation, ask yourself one question: "What would I do if this person were my good friend?" Very soon the word *if* will be gone. With this in mind, the Seven Magic Steps possess a special energy.

Your credo is clear: Treat your customer like a friend, and she will become one.

The magic continues. Your sales numbers grow...
Your friends give your foes a powerful blow.

Magic Step 3

Blast Off with the Big Things

Blast off! Your customer relationships skyrocket.

You want to make this image a reality as quickly as possible with each of your customers. You have previously expressed your intention to provide them with the best service they have ever received. By blasting off with the big things early on, you transform your words into actions. You launch the Best Service Ever...Guaranteed plan. Instantly you establish a basis for credibility, trust, and friendship.

Day-to-day events blur and fade with time. Experiences that make a big impact on your customers ultimately stick in their minds. Magic Step 3 enables you to impress your customers by creating an everlasting imprint.

Reverse a Negative

Occasionally you are faced with customers who have problems with your products or services—a negative situation. With the following technique, you have the opportunity to turn this around into something positive.

Hunger for Problems

Your competitors shake in their shoes at the thought of a customer having a big problem. You, however, hunger for this situation. You crave it. You get downright excited about this opportunity because you know that resolving a problem for a customer may be the supreme way to blast off. A couple of studies strongly support this theory.

The Gallup Organization did an extensive study on the effects that customer problems have on future business. It recorded the percentage of times that customers would purchase again from companies and recommend them to their friends. Here are the results:

Circumstance	Percentage That Would Buy Again or Recommend
Problem and complaint: Not resolved	24 percent
Problem and no complaint	45 percent
All customers	64 percent
Problem and complaint: Resolved	85 percent

As you can see, customers who complained about a problem that wasn't resolved had an abysmal percentage buy-again and recommend rate. Interestingly, the customers who experienced a problem that was resolved had a higher percentage than the category of all customers. This is noteworthy because the category includes some customers who didn't have any problems with the supplier.

Furthermore, a study discussed in the audiocassette tape series *Guerrilla Selling—Live* by Orvel Ray Wilson says that if a problem is resolved quickly, the percentage of repeat buying rises to 95 percent. Solving customers' problems clearly strengthens customer loyalty.

Why does solving problems make such a huge impact on customers? For starters, most reps and companies handle problems so poorly that customers dread dealing with them. The hassle of trying to get a problem solved is often more stressful than the problem itself. Many reps blame other people; they fault their companies for acting too slowly; they claim the problems are not their responsibility; they even blame the customers.

Solving problems effectively separates the great reps from the wannabes. When customers are stressed and you turn the situation around, you give your customers desserts (*stressed* spelled backward is *desserts*). You have converted their pain to pleasure. The bigger the problem is, the bigger is the impact.

Here is an example of blasting off by solving a big problem.

Jim Heath, a sales rep for a Canon, was not happy. His largest customer, Toal Custom Graphics, was having big problems with an expensive, state-of-the-art copier. Toal Custom Graphics provided graphic art services and relied heavily on this copier. The Canon service engineer had made weekly visits for repairs for the past few months. The inconvenience was creating stress and dragging productivity down.

Carol Bowen, the manager of this location, was not pleased. Some of her biggest customers were upset with their response time and were threatening to go to the nearest competitor. Carol's boss, the owner of the Toal Custom Graphics franchise, applied significant pressure on her to rectify the situation—or else. She spoke with Jim and shared her displeasure in no uncertain terms.

Jim apologized and took full responsibility for the resolution. He was calm, confident, and reassuring, and gave Carol his commitment that he would have an action plan for her by the end of the day.

Jim cleared his schedule for the day and spoke with numerous people at Canon headquarters, escalating his calls to upper-level management. Within a few hours, he faxed an action plan to Carol.

Shortly after, the three top technical wizards at Canon headquarters arrived at Carol's door. They had jumped on the first available flight. Jim picked them up from the airport and drove them to the destination. They arrived at 4:30 P.M., and Carol gave them her blessing to work past closing time.

The technical team worked straight through the night, and Jim was there every step of the way. The technical team valued his moral support and appreciated his runs to the local convenience store for food. In the troubleshooting, they finally found the source of the problem. It was so rare that there was only one other documented circumstance like it before.

When Carol walked through the door at 8:00 A.M., the technical team had just inked the last sentence of the repair report. Carol was astounded. She could tell they had worked all night. When Jim informed Carol that the problem was solved, she was ecstatic.

Carol is still doing business with Jim, years later. In addition, Jim has over twenty new customers as a direct result of Carol's sharing this story with others.

Jim was hungry to solve a problem, and he blasted off big time. Jim secured a very loyal customer.

Is the Customer Always Right?

Here, finally, is the definitive answer to the age-old and oft-debated question about whether the customer is always right: Who cares!

Have you ever experienced a situation in which a customer perceived that there was a problem when, in your mind, rational reasoning indicated no problem whatsoever? Did you correct your customer? Your competitors do that routinely. Contradicting your customers may make you feel smart, but it is not a wise sales strategy.

Here is the rule: *If the customer perceives there is a problem, there is one!* Solve it and be a hero. Be happy that the customer gave you the opportunity, however unwarranted it appears.

Take this a step further. In your conversations with your customers, try to catch them when they're right. Acknowledge them for it. Agree with customers whenever possible.

The words you speak can make a difference. If you must correct a customer who has made a statement that is not factual, say, "Actually, ..." instead of: "No, that is not true." Rather than "Yes, but...," try "Yes, and ..." The *but* erases the *yes* in the customer's ears. I always try to keep my *but* out of it.

Spend zero time determining if the customer is right in asking for the problem to be resolved. Invest all of your intensity taking action to resolve the problem. Remember the Gallup statistics: Only 24 percent of customers with unresolved complaints bought again. There was no statistic for how many of them were right.

This short story illustrates the point vividly:

Dennis McCarty was a new sales rep with a company called Lasers Edge that made lasers that construction companies used for alignment and leveling of their construction lots. These devices had a wide range in price. O'Driscoll Construction had purchased one from the previous rep, Mike, a year before for about $10,000.

It had been in for repair twice, and each repair cost about $200. With the frequency that O'Driscoll used it, this was clearly better than the average rate of repair compared to those of similar usage, but Lori Kmet, O'Driscoll's office manager and purse-string holder, didn't see it that way. She thought one repair per year at a maximum was acceptable. Mike had previously informed her of the company policy for repairs and told her he couldn't do anything about it. Although his products were clearly superior to the others on the market, he never got another penny in business from Lori after that original purchase. His competitors got plenty.

When Dennis met Lori, she informed him that she hated his company. Lori explained that she was all too aware of Lasers Edge company policy and asked Dennis to spare her the agony of hearing it again. She proclaimed that she would never buy another laser from Lasers Edge.

The next day Lori received a check for $225, which was the cost of one repair plus a generous interest calculation, along with a short note of apology from Dennis, who promised to help her if she had any further problems. He also arranged through his vice president of service to send out the senior service engineer to do a preventative maintenance check on her laser.

To make a long story short, O'Driscoll Construction purchased over $75,000 in lasers over the course of the next two years.

Was the customer right? Not according to Mike. He knew the policy and the statistics: O'Driscoll's repair rate was better than average. In Mike's words, Lori was simply a "whiny baby" and not worth the effort. Mike let the emotions about knowing she was "wrong" affect his actions.

Dennis's perspective was different. He purposely avoided thinking about whether Lori was right or wrong. He simply focused on solving her problem and gained $75,000 in new business with a $226 (includes the cost of an apology note and stamp) investment and a few minutes of his time. I wish all of my investments yielded such results!

Seven Magic Keys to Problem Solving

These Seven Magic Keys turn on the ignition to your rocket. They guarantee a successful blast-off.

Key 1: Listen

A customer who is upset wants to tell someone about it. The worst thing to do is cut her off before she starts venting. There is no solution in the world that can make her happy if there is still steam in her head. That pent-up steam physically blocks her hearing. No message gets through from her ear to her brain. Listening intently, as long as it takes, opens the vent to release the steam.

Key 2: Empathize

The customer expects a battle when she calls you with a problem. She typically receives resistance at minimum and sometimes even rudeness. When you empathize with her by responding, "I bet that ticked you off!" or "How frustrating!" suddenly you are on the same team. It's no longer her against you; it's both of you against the problem.

Be careful not to disparage your company with comments such as, "Yeah, our Customer Service Department is clueless!" This is a counterproductive sales strategy. Empathize. Don't criticize.

Key 3: Apologize

They say music can soothe the savage beast. In sales, an apology can soothe the savage customer. Perhaps the two most powerful words you can utter in this situation are "I apologize." The results are instantaneous and dramatic. The customer's facial expression often shows it, and a sigh of relief is sometimes audible. You have liberated that last pocket of steam.

Why is an apology so effective? Few reps actually do it. Customers seldom hear reps admit they or their companies made a mistake. Sometimes all the customer really is looking for is an apology. There may not be a solution. The apology itself can be the solution.

Accept responsibility even if it is not your fault. Never say, "It's not my job" or "It's not my responsibility." Those phrases are certain to infuriate any customer.

After you apologize, your customers often tell you it's not your fault. Your response to them is, "Perhaps the problem is not my fault. Regardless, I most certainly accept full responsibility to resolve the situation to your complete satisfaction."

Key 4: Reassure

Now that your customer has settled down, you need to reassure her that you will solve her problem. If you show panic, your customer will panic too. Your demeanor transfers to your customer. Notice I have chosen my words carefully. Substituting the word *feel* for *show* would be inaccurate. You may very well *feel* frantic. Just don't *show* it. Show calmness and confidence. At an appropriate time, consider the use of humor to break the tension and lighten the atmosphere.

Key 5: Throw Out the Book

Toss the policy book, because now anything goes. No idea is too extreme. It is fatal to tell a customer you can't do something because it is "against our policy." That is the granddaddy of them all, certain to make a customer irate. Rather, relentlessly pursue a solution drawing on all of your resources to satisfy your customer. Working all night wasn't in the Canon policy book. Satisfying the customer was.

Key 6: Use an Action Plan

An action plan is essential. It provides organization, accountability, credibility, teamwork, and speed. In fact, an effective plan in writing provides instant credibility. The written word is extremely powerful.

Act immediately to determine the plan. If a problem lingers, it festers into a bigger problem and allows more time for upset customers to tell their friends how mad they are. In Magic Step 3, you discover that solving a problem quickly can elevate customer retention to 95 percent. Heed that advice.

You also need to determine these key parameters:

Problem. Agreeing on exactly what the problem is can often be an overlooked element in the process. It is fundamental to define the problem first.

Success. It is just as important to determine what success means to the customer. As you learned from Magic Step 1, don't guess what it will take to satisfy the customer. Ask! You could launch what you think is an awesome plan, yet incur a colossal waste of time, energy, and money if the solution you are shooting for is unacceptable to the customer. You must also agree that you can achieve success by her definition. If the customer's definition of success is not realistically achievable, inform her accordingly. At that point, agree to a different course of action.

Action: Who and by When. Frequently you should involve additional resources in developing and executing the plan. Thus, it is imperative to determine who will perform each action and by when it will be completed. Timeliness of the resolution is thereby ensured, and accountability is built into the plan. Work as a team with individual responsibility for actions.

When you choose people to be on this team, make sure that you pick the top people from each department. If you don't know who they are, network internally to find out. Your customers should always work with the top talent from your organization. It is your responsibility to ensure this happens.

Review the action plan with your customers, and ask for their participation, noting their actions in the written action plan. Including the customer as a member of the problem-solving team puts you on the same team instead of opposing sides.

One of the actions will be a review meeting. Establish a date when the team will meet again. In that meeting, review progress, and adjust the action plan accordingly. The process continues until the customer is satisfied.

Exhibit 1 shows an example of an action plan, this one for Toal Custom Graphics. Feel free to use this format or create your own. The length of the plan varies based on the nature of the problem.

Key 7: Send Thank-You—Plus

Once you have resolved the problem to your customer's complete satisfaction, send a thank-you letter that thanks the customer for her patience and loyalty. Customer loyalty means a ton, and you want your customers to know it. The letter that Dennis McCarty sent to Lori Kmet at Lasers Edge is shown in Exhibit 2.

In addition, send a small token of your appreciation catered to the customer's preference. If you don't already know what this might be, ask a secretary or business associate for suggestions. The cost of the gift depends on what the individual customer would find appropriate. Jim Heath sent a gift certificate to Carol Bowen to her favorite restaurant for her to enjoy with her husband. Dennis sent a box of Lori's favorite chocolate-covered turtles. The cost is less important than the custom selection of the gift.

This approach may give the customer the feeling that she came out ahead in the deal. Her problem is gone, *plus* she has this nice gift.

Problem: Color copier has been down for repair too frequently. The copier has been serviced five times in the past two months.

Success: A repair rate on the Toal Custom Graphics copier of three times per year or less.

Action	Who	By When
Assemble technical team.	J. Heath	7/27
Research the repair history database for similar circumstances to determine potential solutions. Report to Team.	Tech Support	7/27
Provide after-hours access to the Toal Custom Graphics facility.	Carol	7/27
Inspect, troubleshoot, and repair copier.	Tech Team	7/27
Review repair report.	Tech Team, Jim, Carol	7/28
Review meeting— to assess and ensure satisfaction. Determine date of next review meeting.	Tech Team, Jim, Carol	8/28
Monitor Toal Custom Graphics' repair reports as they occur.	Lead Tech	Ongoing
Review annual repair summary.	Jim, Carol	End of each year

Exhibit 1. Toal Custom Graphics action plan.

September 11, 20xx

Ms. Lori Kmet
O'Driscoll Construction
1221 Sixth Street
Marshall, Michigan 49068

Dear Lori:
    I apologize for the frustration you have experienced recently with the repairs on your laser. A repair rate higher than your expectations is unacceptable.
    I have informed the Vice President of Service at Lasers Edge. He will be sending out our Senior Service Engineer to do a preventative maintenance check on your laser. We will ensure that your laser is performing in top-quality fashion.
    I am hopeful that soon you will be completely satisfied with your Lasers Edge laser. If there is ever anything I can do to help, please notify me immediately. You may reach me at the following numbers:
    Home Number: (616) 955–6565
    Pager Number: (888) 280–3370
    As a small token of my appreciation of your patience, I have enclosed this gift. A friend in your office informed me that you enjoy these.

Sincerely,

Dennis McCarty

Exhibit 2. Thank you–plus letter.

Now that you have the Seven Magic Keys in your pocket, use them most effectively by promising to take problems off your customers' hands on their first phone call. Even if the difficulty is the fault of an obscure division of a corporation that you don't even work for based in a remote country, take care of it for your customers.

Customers are painfully accustomed to making several calls before navigating through "voice-mail jail" to speak with a person. It requires numerous calls before they finally get results. If customers know they can make one phone call to have their problems solved, which route do you think they choose?

Great friendships are interdependent. You depend on your customers to provide a living for yourself and your family. In turn, your customers need to depend on you. Each time you deliver when a customer trusts you to solve a problem, your friendship grows.

As customers' dependence on you increases, the types of "problems" they bring to you expand. You start to receive calls asking, "Could you please help me with a problem? My _____ from your competitor is on its last leg. I think I need to replace it. What would you recommend?"

Too bad your competitors don't have time to deal with problems!

Seize a Positive

It is January. It is Michigan. A blizzard is coming tomorrow. Such is life in a Michigan winter. Schools close. Kids get to make snowmen and go sledding. Businesses close. Adults get to make snowmen and go sledding. The streets are virtually vacant.

Dana Verville is not happy. It's not that he dislikes snowmen and sledding. In fact, he builds a pretty good snowman. Unfortunately, tomorrow is the day of his big product evaluation, and the hospital is 180 miles away from his home. Dana has never done business with this hospital. No one else in his company ever has either. The lead plastic surgeon, Dr. Deem, has a facial reconstruction surgery scheduled and plans to evaluate Dana's new surgical instruments. But the patient can't wait, so the surgery will not be canceled.

Dr. Deem understands that Dana will need to reschedule because of the weather, so he will use the same surgical instruments that he has been using all along.

Not a chance! Dana seizes this opportunity to blast off. He borrows his buddy's four-wheel drive and leaves home the night before the storm hits town. He stays in a hotel near the hospital.

The next morning he arrives at the hospital—early. He greets Dr. Deem as he enters the surgery department. Dr. Deem is about thirty minutes late due to the stormy conditions. An astonished yet pleased look lights up his face when he sees Dana.

The surgery goes exceptionally well. Dr. Deem likes Dana's surgical instruments, and he loves Dana's commitment.

The storm rages on. Dana stays the night—at Dr. Deem's house! He enjoys a nice dinner with the family and an HBO movie to follow. He heads home in the morning after the weather clears.

In less than forty-eight hours, Dana catapulted from a nobody to a hero. As you may have guessed, he won the business, and he has never looked back. His sales revenues have grown considerably across his other product lines, and his competitors say he "owns that hospital."

Boom! What a blast-off!

You can judge from the length of this section that the strategy is rather simple: Seize any opportunity you can find to make a positive impact on your customers by taking action well beyond common expectations. The opportunities are endless. The key is to look closely to recognize them. Wherever you see an opening, pounce on it.

Blast-off is a lock.

Use Formal Agreements

If you execute the Seven Magic Steps properly, why would you need a formal agreement? The answer is, you wouldn't—that is, if personnel and circumstances at your accounts never change. Unfortunately, that is not a reality. Key decision makers often get promoted or take positions with other companies. If a new person arrives who had a terrible previous experience with your company, you could lose your business in a blink.

Formal agreements act to support the other principles of the Seven Magic Steps. They certainly don't serve as a substitute for them. In the absence of great relationships, these agreements carry less strength. In the presence of strong friendships, formal agreements solidify your business beyond any faint hope of your competitors.

Obviously, sales reps can be persuasive at times. These agreements give your customers an easy way to say no and stop your competitors in their tracks before they launch into their spiels. It clearly reduces the pestering your customers receive, and secures your business at the same time—a win for both of you.

What if your company doesn't have formal agreements for your use? Don't panic; my company doesn't either. Remember that this book is targeted to sales representatives, so the focus is on actions that you can enact. This is one of them.

Exhibit 3 contains an example agreement for your use. I created this on my own rather than waiting for my corporation to do it. As an added benefit, my sister reviewed the document. She is a lawyer and a darn good one. The agreement is sound and binding.

It is wise to gain your company's support and approval for this agreement. Their support will be beneficial, and their approval will keep you employed, although it is unlikely anyone would provide resistance. The agreements most assuredly are in the best interest of the company.

Wait. This chapter is about blasting off with your customers. How do formal agreements make a big positive impact on your customers?

Usually they don't. In fact, some make a negative impact. Most companies call their agreements "contracts." That word alone scares customers. Customers commonly perceive that the contracts are designed to protect the companies' interests. They think they are written in legalese designed to trick them into undesired consequences. Customers believe they are written for the exclusive benefit of the companies. For these reasons, many customers won't sign contracts of this nature.

The success factor to your agreements is that they are mutually beneficial. Use normal, everyday English instead of legalese to avoid customer suspicion. Clearly spell out the benefits your customers receive. Then state the specific rewards that your company obtains.

Kahn Enterprises, 100 Washington Dr. S.E., Grand Rapids, MI 49506, and the Lauria Corporation, 4100 E. Milham, Kalamazoo, MI 49001 enter into the Customer Friendship Agreement which shall be subject to the following conditions:

1. Duration of Agreement

This agreement shall become effective on January 1, 2001, and shall continue in effect for a period of three years.

2. Terms

A. Fixed Pricing

There will be no price increases above the current level for any product purchased from the Lauria Corporation for the entire term of the agreement.

B. Customer Friendship Points

Kahn Enterprises will earn free product from Lauria Corporation through the purchase of Lauria Corporation products. For each $100 of Lauria Corporation products purchased, Kahn Enterprises will earn two points. For each $100 of Lauria Corporation products purchased above the amount purchased in the previous year, Kahn Enterprises will earn a total of four points. At the end of the year, Kahn Enterprises may exchange each point for one dollar credit for purchases of Lauria Corporation products.

C. Inventory

Lauria Corporation will place all of Kahn Enterprises inventory on consignment at no charge.

D. Education Program

Lauria Corporation will sponsor three Kahn Enterprises employees to attend the National Auto Body Educational Seminar each year. Lauria Corporation will pay all expenses.

E. Customer Friendship Visit

Lauria Corporation will invite three Kahn Enterprises employees to attend a Customer Friendship Visit at the Lauria Corporation. Lauria Corporation will pay all expenses.

F. Customer Loyalty

Kahn Enterprises agrees to exclusively purchase Lauria Corporation products that are on pages 2–30 of the 2001 catalogue.

G. Customer Reference

Kahn Enterprises agrees to speak with and allow visits from other potential Lauria Corporation customers.

(Name/Title)
Kahn Enterprises

(Name/Title)
Lauria Corporation

(Date)

(Date)

Exhibit 3. Customer Friendship Agreement.

Calling them "contracts" is a kiss of death. Rather, call them Customer Friendship Agreements, a term with positive connotations. The word *friendship* implies that commitment is given willingly, not by forced obligation. It signifies that there is something in it for both parties rather than just one (the wrong one). The name knocks down the barriers that the word *contract* places between the customer and company. It is warm, yet it calls for the strongest bond possible: friendship. The word *customer* reminds you that this strong relationship still involves the exchange of business.

Let's address what benefits your customers receive. Customize the customer friendships to the unique needs of the individual customer. Include attributes that generate great value in each customer's eyes. Elevate customers on pedestals to create the feeling that they are special to you, because they are.

This is where you blast off.

There are several customer benefits listed below that you may choose to include in your Customer Friendship Agreements. Some you can implement on your own. Others you need to involve other company team members to execute. The possibilities are limitless. These suggestions will spur other inventive ideas that you can add to the list.

Customer Friendship Benefits to the Customer

- Pricing
  - Provide additional discount.
  - Freeze pricing for the term of the agreement.
  - Offer incremental discounting as the customer buys more of your product lines.
- Shipping
  - Reduce the cost of shipping.
  - Improve the speed of shipping (i.e., offer overnight delivery instead of ground shipping).

- Inventory
  - Place customer inventory on consignment. The product supply on the customer's shelves would be on your books, not theirs.
- Payment terms
  - Extend terms from thirty days to sixty days.
- Financing
  - Give reduced or no interest financing.
- Rebate
  - The customer earns points for dollars spent on your products.
  - Points may be redeemed for free product or other perks.
- Loaners
  - Provide loaner equipment for free when customer equipment is in for repair.
- Service
  - Commit to improved response time.
  - Give an additional level of service that is more comprehensive.
- Education
  - Include on-site educational seminars.
  - Sponsor the customer to attend an off-site educational event of her choice.
- Expert
  - Bring an expert to visit the customer to analyze a specific facet of the company and provide recommendations for improvement.
  - Use an expert from your company or a third party.
- Focus group
  - Invite the customer to participate in a focus group—perhaps one about new product designs or new services.
- Customer friendship visit
  - Fly the customer to the company headquarters.
  - Provide first-class airline, hotel, transportation (limousine), and restaurant accommodations.

- Involve company personnel at all levels, including the CEO.
- Give a "tour of the house." It is your turn to show your "house" to your customer friends.
- Product customizing
    - Manufacture products customized to the customer's needs.
    - Put the customer's logo on the products.
- Computer systems
    - Link customer and company computer systems.
    - Give the customer access to production schedules, back orders, and other relevant information.

Clearly a customer agreement that includes a selection of these rewards makes a blast-off impact. Some ideas toward the bottom of the list require sizable time and money investments and might best be geared for customers with enough revenue to justify them.

A word of caution in determining whether the investment is justifiable. Focus groups give customers a feeling of ownership. When they see their ideas ultimately become products, those products become theirs. A competitor doesn't have a chance in this situation. A consultation with an expert could encourage an improvement that yields huge dividends.

The success rate of customer friendship visits is phenomenal. A bond of friendship is created unlike any other. The following story illustrates this point vividly.

Pat Leonard, a superb sales rep, works for a corporation that makes supplies for home repair stores. He handles the large, national accounts.

Home Depot put a major contract for its entire chain up for bid a couple years ago. Supply companies salivated at the thought of the opportunity and assembled their best sales teams for this endeavor.

Team after team visited Home Depot's headquarters to meet with the top executives. Fancy product demonstrations, price structures, and delivery plans comprised the routine presentation. All were impressive.

Pat knew he had to differentiate his approach. Instead of traveling to Home Depot's site, he invited the top executives from headquarters and the ten largest stores to visit his corporation's headquarters in Boston. None of his competitors had these guests in their audience.

To say he rallied his team to make the trip special for the Home Depot executives is the understatement of the century. Stretch limos awaited them at the airport. Upon arrival at their five-star hotel, they found gift baskets in their rooms with fruit, snacks, and drinks. They also included lobster Beanie Babies labeled with their children's names.

To top it off, a FedEx box prelabeled with each person's home address sat next to the baskets. The note inside read, "Thank you for letting your mommy/daddy play with us today. Give this lobster a big hug and think of how much you love your mommy/daddy. She/He will be home with you soon." The customers added a short note of their own if they wished and then dropped the box off at the front desk to be sent home overnight.

The hot topic at dinner that evening, of course, was the gifts. Pat had learned of all special food requests in advance of the trip and coordinated with the restaurant. The atmosphere was festive and the conversation casual. Not once did the topic of business arise. This was a group of friends having a wonderful time together.

To the executives' surprise, when they arrived at headquarters, every person in the building was wearing a button that said Welcome Friends from Home Depot. The environment was electric with the excitement of this momentous visit.

Sure, Pat's team presented product, price, and delivery information. Unlike their competitors, they also keenly focused on the importance of strong relationships and stellar service.

Pat secured a five-year, multimillion dollar agreement.

Here is the list of what's in it for you.

Customer Friendship Benefits to the Company

- *Loyalty.* The customer agrees to use your products exclusively for the term of the agreement.
- *Reference.* The customer speaks with prospective customers as a positive reference for your company.

- *New Ideas.* Your marketing and development staffs receive input on new product designs or new services from focus groups. Who knows better than the end users how to innovate and improve your offerings?
- *Efficiency Increases.* By partnering closely with your customer on production schedules and inventory positions, your planning and efficiency improve.

The gain for you from this relatively short list is tremendous. Your customers agree to use only your products and to tell the world how great you are. Your back door is secure. They provide you with new ideas, make you more efficient, buy your products, and then sell them to others. What better commitment could you ask for?

The length of the agreement varies based on the individual customer. Three years typically is a good place to start. Which customers should you choose for customer friendships? The top two? Top ten? Top half? Nope. All of them.

Recall the Magic Formula: $7 - 0 = 1$. Are there any customers whose business you don't want to solidify for the long term? Probably not. The primary concern is your investment of resources. How could you find time to do this with all of your customers? Could you justify the expense? The answer again is to customize each agreement. Do not offer all of these options to all of your customers. Perhaps offer some of your smaller customers just a few of the benefits that require minimal concessions and effort on your part. You may choose to give your largest customers the majority of these benefits.

Involve all the personnel at each customer account in your customer friendships. Ensure that you have loyal relationships throughout the entire account. In a flash, a line employee can be promoted to a management position. If you have shunned that person, your business could instantly be in jeopardy.

In terms of the meetings and discussions that occur between the company and customer personnel, it just isn't practical to have every employee involved. The goal is to have as many as reasonably possible directly participate.

You have a plan for those who are unable to join in those meetings. On the day you jointly commit to the Customer Friendship, have a celebration with the entire company. Announce the Customer Friendship and review the benefits (that aren't confidential). Share ice cream sundaes, cake, beer, champagne, or whatever else is appropriate to celebrate with that customer (see Magic Step 4 for more ideas).

Celebrate again each year on the anniversary of the Customer Friendship. This gives you the opportunity to remind everyone of the partnership. Communicate specific results that each party has achieved so far. Then review potential business opportunities for the coming year. Call this the Customer Friendship Anniversary Review.

Take a moment to ponder what happens when your competitor visits your customer attempting to steal your business. What a pleasant vision to reflect on.

The Magic continues. Your sales numbers grow...
Blast-off occurred a minute ago!

Magic Step 4

Light 'Em Up with the Little Things

Her face beamed with brightness as she smiled from head to toe. Instantly, her day just became a little better.

This is the description of a customer who was lit up by a sales rep who was doing the little things for her. By little things, I mean taking small actions designed to light up your customers. Consciously focus on making their day a little brighter than before you interacted with them.

The beauty of doing the little things is that the impact can be just as powerful as doing the big things. The primary difference is in the amount of effort required. The investment of time is minimal, but the return is tremendous.

Intentionally making customers feel better is operating on an entirely different level than your competitors do. They are often concerned merely with features and benefits. They don't want to waste time on something that doesn't have an immediate effect on a specific order.

You now know the value of strong friendships with customers and the resulting loyalty you gain. You have experienced how much easier and faster sales progress when you work with friends. As relationships get stronger, sales cycles get shorter.

Your competitors are right. The following ideas will not affect a specific order. Rather, they will affect all of your future orders.

Send Cards

People enjoy receiving cards. Not many things in life are universal. This one is as close as it gets. Receiving a card in the mail brightens your day. The impact is always there, and sometimes it's a big one.

My customer's name was Gretchen Black, and she was not very nice to me. One day that I met with her, she was particularly ornery. I asked her if she was having a tough day. She curtly responded with an emphatic yes. That our meeting was brief was the only good part about it.

Most reps would have followed their natural reactions: walk to the car mumbling expletives about her, and vow never to call on her again. Taking the opposite approach, I sent her a card the next day. It was one of those clever cards found in the "Cheer Up" or "Cope" sections of the card shop that make humor out of stressful situations. I wrote her a short, sincere note in the card. I said I was sorry she had such a bad day and wished her better times ahead.

It took me a grand total of three minutes to send this card. The effect it had on Gretchen was 100 times greater than anything I had done in the previous three years.

The next time she saw me, she came up to me in the hallway. The fact that she approached me was notable itself. I typically had to attempt an open-field tackle just to get her to slow down enough to speak with me. She had pretty good speed too! She looked me dead in the eye and with a sincere smile thanked me for the card. She told me it had really brightened her day.

I was shocked! I had never seen her smile before. Our relationship was never the same again. Thank goodness. She became friendly, sincere, and unshakably loyal. It was well worth three minutes of my time.

The key to being excellent at sending cards is buying in bulk. Buy fifty cards at a time covering a variety of occasions. Stop at the post office and acquire several rolls of stamps. This takes one trip. You just saved forty-nine trips to the card store and forty-nine more to the post office.

Many people think of sending a card but don't follow through. They ponder going to the store to pick out a card and then to the post office for stamps. They figure it will take at least a half-hour to finish the task. They don't have a half-hour, so it doesn't happen.

Here are some card types to stock up on:

- *Cheer up.* Gretchen isn't the only one to have a bad day on occasion. With the rising stress levels in business, this happens more frequently than ever before.
- *Congratulations.* Look for any opportunity to send congratulation cards. It feels great to be congratulated. You want to share in your customers' victories.
- *Sympathy.* These customers are your friends. If someone close to them dies, sending a sympathy card is the minimum you should do. Perhaps flowers or a personal visit to the funeral home may be appropriate.
- *Thank You.* Thank your customers often, both verbally and in print. A thank-you note out of the blue just for being your customer is a nice touch. Including a sincere compliment gives it a boost.
- *Birthday.* How do you remember all those birthdays? You don't have to. Put them in your organizational system. Whether you use a planner or a computer program, note each birthday in the same fashion as other business action items. It is helpful to put the entry a week ahead of the birthday to give the mail time to get there.
- *Holiday.* This occasion is more obligatory than it is novel. Many people send Christmas cards, so it is more likely that your customers will notice if you don't send them rather than if you do.

My suggestion is to send cards that say "Happy Holidays" rather than "Merry Christmas" if you don't know the customer's religion.

- *Create Your Own.* There are software programs for home computers that allow you to create your own cards (one of them is Print Shop by Broderbund). These offer a fast, easy way to customize cards for the individual customers.

- *E-Mail Cards.* Similar to the software programs, you may send customized cards efficiently via e-mail. Simply search under "e-cards" to find numerous options, including some that are free.

Don't be surprised to find these cards prominently displayed in your customers' offices. They often feel proud to show off the fact that one of their friends cared enough to send them a card.

Make Their Lives Easier

Help your customers in any way possible to make their business and personal lives easier. Your competitors help their customers only with business issues that have a direct influence on their sales. That is shortsighted.

You have strong training, talents, and connections in certain areas that your customers may not. Use these strengths to do favors for your customers.

Let's say your customer informs you that a key item from another company is on back order. She needs it urgently but will have to wait. False! You know how companies operate. Many of them have emergency stashes of stock. Call the product manager, vice president, the owner, or whoever the person is with the key to the emergency supply. If the company really is completely out of stock, request the names and phone numbers of other customers who purchase the same product. Call them, and ask if you can borrow some product.

That is just one example of many ways to help your customers with their business needs that don't directly relate to you. The same concept applies to personal assistance.

Jimmy Polacko, a good friend of mine, told me of a time he helped his customer Erin Byrne buy a cellular phone. She had never purchased a cellular phone before and was justifiably uneasy about the process. Jimmy, who had purchased many cellular phones over the years, found the best phone for Erin based on her needs and negotiated an excellent deal for her: The store waived the activation charge, the phone itself was free instead of $99, and the commitment term was two years instead of three.

He brought the agreement to Erin for her signature, then took it to the phone dealer and returned to her with phone in hand. She never stepped foot in the store. She experienced no anxiety, stress, or outright fear. Erin's smile came from the heart and filled the room. Jimmy's self-less actions made a permanent impression on her.

How do your customers feel when you go out of your way to make their lives easier? Awesome—about themselves and about you!

Remember Names

Let's play Jeopardy. The answer will be given. You have to guess the question.

Answer: I am just not good with names.

Did you guess the question? Here it is:

Question: What is the biggest cop-out excuse of all time that sales reps use?

To say that you don't have the mental capacity to remember names is both weak and unfounded. If you have the intellect to read this book, you clearly have the ability to be excellent with names. There are no bad memories, only bad efforts.

If someone offered you $1,000 to remember the name of the next person you met, would you remember that name? That cash would be in your pocket faster than I can type this sentence regardless of how bad you may have previously thought you were with names. It's just a matter of how much you want to remember them.

My close friend Lorri Rhoda called on Western Allied Interiors for the first time in March. Putting her Seven Magic Steps into action, she took a "tour of the house" with John Sommerdyke, the office manager, and was introduced to the office staff of ten people. She completed her visit and scheduled a follow up-appointment for a month later.

When Lorri returned to Western Allied, she greeted each of the ten people she met—by name. It had been an entire month since Lorri had met them, and they collectively were dazzled. They were touched and impressed by the fact that Lorri cared enough to remember their names. Suddenly the atmosphere became friendly and warm. Bill Kelly, their supplier for the past three years, only called John and a few of the others by name. The rest must not have been important enough—or perhaps he was "just not good with names."

Lorri came back for a third time the next week. Again, she greeted each by name, and each called Lorri by hers. Smiles lighted their faces as they were genuinely happy to see her. She was now one of the gang. Lorri won the business on that third visit. What took Bill three years to build Lorri conquered in three calls.

Did Lorri get the business only because she remembered their names? No. Was it a key catalyst? Yes.

Remembering names may be the single most significant step toward a friendship. Yet it may also be the least effective skill of the majority of sales reps.

Think of when you were in a social situation and someone failed to remember your name. It felt awkward and uncomfortable. You felt less important, less valued, less significant than the others in the room whom this person called by name. You experienced resentment toward this person. You have not forgotten the fact that this person once forgot your name.

In turn, you impress people when you remember names. Most people struggle with names and are surprised to find someone who is good at it. You show them that they are worth the effort. You pay tribute to them. You validate them as important persons when you call them by name.

As an additional benefit, when you remember someone's name, that person feels obligated to remember yours. The atmosphere changes when you walk into a room greeting everyone by name, and everyone calls you by name in return. The relationship suddenly is rooted on friendly ground.

How do you master this skill?

It is critical to convert the negative thoughts into positive energy. Erase the ever famous cop-out from your mind. If you tell yourself that you are excellent with names, you will be. Your confidence with names will snowball. Soon you'll look forward to introductions rather than dreading them.

Once you have the proper mind-set, master what I call the Magic Seven seconds. If you lock the name in during the first Magic Seven seconds, you will remember it forever. Consciously focus on the person's name and embed it in your memory during this time span. If you don't lock it in by the time seven seconds are up, that name will likely be lost for good. This sounds easy, so why do so many people struggle with names?

Many other distracting thoughts run through your mind when you meet someone new. You might think of their looks. Perhaps you wonder what they are thinking about you. You might focus on the chive stuck on someone's tooth from dinner. A million different thoughts could cross your mind. The key is to block those distracting thoughts from your mind and focus on locking the person's name into memory.

During the Magic Seven seconds, you need to do two things:

1. *Say the person's name two times when you meet him.* That may sound a bit dorky, but there is an easy way to do this and not sound dorky at all. When the person states his name, say his name in return. If the name is an easy one, say the name in the form of a statement. If it is tricky, say the name in the form of a question to confirm that you are pronouncing it correctly. Then tell him you are happy to meet him as you repeat his name. For example:

"Hi. My name is Dave."
"Dave, I'm Tim. It is a pleasure to meet you, Dave."

or

"Hi. My name is Bryce."
"Bryce? [Bryce acknowledges that is correct.] I'm Tim. It is a pleasure to meet you, Bryce."

Saying the name twice facilitates the memory lock. It brings your attention to the name and away from other diversions. By the way, always say the name as the person says it to help avoid a common mistake. If the person says "Robert," you say "Robert," not "Bob." People introduce themselves as they want to be addressed. You may offend them if you change the name in any way.

2. *Use picture association.* When you first hear the person's name, pick something that this name brings to mind— an object, a place, or a famous person. For example, you might think of an angel for the name Angela. For Joe, the famous GI Joe toy fits the bill.

Now associate this picture with the most distinguishing feature of the person. Sticking with the examples, let's say Angela has large, pretty eyes. You would envision an angel in each of Angela's eyes. Then take a mental picture of this association, and implant the picture in your memory. Joe has large ears. You might form a mental picture of GI Joe using his kung fu grip to hold onto Joe's ear. The more ridiculous the vision is, the easier it is to recall. When you see that person again, recall the picture you created.

That person's most distinguishing feature will trigger your memory. So for all those people who "just aren't good with names," here is another way to look at it. With this approach, you don't have to remember names. You remember pictures. This is particularly well suited for those who say, "I'm bad with names, but I never forget a face."

As a measure of insurance, write down the picture association for each person where you keep a record of your customers' names. From the example with Angela, you might write, "Angela— angel/large eyes." Prior to entering an account that you haven't visited recently, review the list of names and associations to bolster your memory.

It may seem like a lot of effort to remember a name, but after some practice, the process becomes second nature. The question is, "Is it worth seven seconds of my time to remember a name?" The answer to that question is an emphatic Yes! especially when you see that person's face after you call her by name a month later. Her face will light up like a Christmas tree.

Smile

A smile can crumble a wall. It can build a bridge. It can brighten a day. And it doesn't cost a penny. Now that's a pretty darn good bargain.

Many reps—in fact, most—do not smile enough. They get so focused on the task at hand that they forget to smile. It is not written in their planner, so they don't do it. They appear distant or even arrogant as a result.

When someone smiles sincerely at you, you feel wonderful. There is something magic about a real smile. It can instantly make someone's disposition happier. A smile can bring a customer's guard down. A smile helps you to make a connection. It is challenging not to smile at someone who smiles at you.

Smile early, and smile often. This is the best way to ensure a good first impression, and you already know how imperative good first impressions are. Smiling when you greet a customer instantly conveys that you are a warm human being instead of a cold sales rep. Smiling throughout the conversation maintains your connection.

This even works on the phone. When you smile while speaking on the phone, the person on the other end can almost feel it. You infuse a noticeable presence of energy into the conversation. It may seem awkward at first, but it becomes natural quickly.

Smiling is underrated and underused—but not by you. Not anymore. A smile lights up a room. Use it to light up your customers.

Mom Always Said: "Use Good Manners"

Good manners are vanishing, and it seems to be getting worse, not better. Observe a group of kids these days. It is far more likely that expletives, not polite conversation, will spout from their mouths.

Using good manners is both polite and charming. It makes a positive impression to say "Please" and "Thank you." Many people say these terms occasionally, without feeling. Few say them routinely, with warmth.

You feel good about helping people when they respond to your request, "Yes, please." It shows that they don't take you for granted. It shows respect.

When a customer tells you she needs help, avoid responses such as: "What's the problem?" which implies "What's your problem, you stupid fool?!" I don't believe this is the message you want to convey to your customers. An effective reply is, "I would be happy to help. Please inform me of the situation." It has a slightly nicer ring to it than the "stupid fool" line.

"Take Off Your Coat ... "

"...and make yourself at home." When a friend comes into your house, you might say this. You want the atmosphere to be casual and comfortable. In Magic Step 2, you read about taking a "tour of the house." The idea here keeps in line with that concept.

Your conversations with your customers should be casual and comfortable as well. When you visit a customer, it is likely that he will have his suit coat off. Most people wear their suit coats to and from work yet seldom during work. It's an odd custom in business.

Follow your customer's lead. Either leave the coat in the car or take it off once you are in his office. Voilà! You look like one of "us" instead of one of "them." One barrier between you has been removed. It is easier for both of you to relax. Suit coats are binding in more ways than one.

Even though your customer isn't wearing a coat, he may not think to ask you to take off yours. This is likely based on habit. The customer is accustomed to seeing reps wearing coats. To be polite, you may choose to ask the customer if he minds if you take your coat off. After all, you are excellent with manners.

There are exceptions to every rule. If your customer is wearing a coat, it is a good idea to keep your coat on. He may prefer a more formal setting. The choice is his, not yours. You must show respect too.

Consider regional and industry issues. When doing business in Hawaii, you are way overdressed if you wear a tie. In the banking world, suit coats (conservative gray preferably) may be appropriate.

If you are a woman, you might be asking, "How does this apply to me?" The concept is the same for women as is it is for men. With business suits that allow it, take off the coat if the customer has his off. As for skirts or dresses, keep the spirit of the concept in mind. Dress at a similar level of casualness as your customer. Eliminate the formal attire barrier.

Keric DeChant, a vice president at the Stryker Corporation, where I'm employed, wears special ties given to him by his kids to important meetings. Winnie the Pooh, Snoopy, and other traditional friends adorn the ties. Customers invariably comment. It gives Keric the opportunity to mention the gifts from his children. Suddenly Keric is a dad, not just a vice president. The barrier vanishes.

You are visiting with friends. Dress accordingly.

Keep Promises

Do you always keep your promises with your customers? The knee-jerk answer is, "Of course." Upon further thought, it really depends on what you consider a promise.

The most literal interpretation of the word *promise* applies only to commitments that you declare assurance with the actual word *promise.* Using that definition, "I promise to get the quote to you this week" is a promise. "I will get the quote to you this week" is not a promise in the literal sense.

Nice try. Unfortunately, your customers don't see it this way, and it's their view that counts, not yours. Any commitment you make becomes a promise in your customers' eyes. To be on the safe side, even if you say you "might" do something, interpret the statement as a promise. Your customers often will. The word *might* drops from their memory. Have you ever experienced this with a customer? Me too.

Anyone with children can relate to this. Telling a customer, "I might be able to get your new computer system to you by Friday," is comparable to telling your five year old, "I might be able to take you for an ice cream cone today." The five-year-old never hears the word *might.* Neither does the customer. The five year old will throw a major tantrum if he doesn't get it. So will the customer. The difference is that you are always the recipient of the child's tantrum, but only sometimes do you see the customer's reaction. The customer may instead vent to friends or work associates. Other times the customer internalizes the reaction. Regardless of how the tantrum occurs, just as certain as the child pitches a fit, so does the customer.

Interpreting all of your commitments to customers as promises to friends makes you reliable in keeping them. Promises are sacred. The ramifications of breaking them are grave.

Many facets of the business world are just not reliable. Copy machines break down right when you need them. Cellular phone conversations disconnect when you are speaking with the CEO. Power surges zap your computer just prior to saving a ten-page project. People say they are going to do something, and they do it late, incorrectly, or not at all.

When your customers can count on you to keep your promises, you give them one less thing to worry about going wrong. You strengthen their trust in you each time you keep a promise.

You lie to your customer if you break a promise. And think about the damage a lie does to your customer's trust in you. Customers do not tolerate broken promises. They may not have the option to get rid of their cellular phone or their computer, but they most certainly can dump you in a nanosecond if you break a single promise.

Good Enough...Isn't

Keeping promises is the price of admission. That gives you the chance to do business with your customers. What you do beyond your promises is how you distance yourself from your competitors.

Many of your competitors adopt a "good enough" attitude: They do just enough to meet the minimal requirements of their commitments and are too busy to do anything extra. They must get to their next stop—urgently. Doing more than the basics slows them down.

Here is a surprising paradox: Many of your competitors give average service to their biggest customers. Wait a minute. How can that be? Why would reps give average service to their biggest customers? The answer is complacency. The "good enough" attitude takes over.

At one time, your competitor delivered great service. That is how he captured the account and developed it to such high levels. But in time, he began to take the account for granted. Now he is busy trying to woo new customers and has fallen back to meeting the minimum requirements. Besides, they have been doing business together for years. He figures that his biggest customer understands.

Wrong!

When you come in and deliver promise-plus service, you blow your competitor's doors off. He won't know what hit him. His biggest customer becomes your loyal friend.

Follow an easy, three-part process.

1. *Build a buffer.* This critically important step is often missed. Give yourself the chance to deliver promise-plus service. If you make a promise that is at your maximum limits, it's not possible to do

any better. If you build a buffer when you make a promise, you give yourself a strong chance to deliver promise-plus service.

The challenge in doing this is that you want to give your customers the best news you can up front. You want to impress them with how well you do your job. Your good intentions, unfortunately, can put you in a bad position. You don't always have complete control over the circumstances. It seems that more often than not, things take longer and cost more than you originally expected. You find yourself struggling just to meet your base commitment. Doing any better than that becomes unachievable.

Train yourself into saving the best for last. The right time to give your customers the good news is after delivering on your original promise, not before.

2. *Ask the customer for acceptance of your commitment.* That is different from telling the customer what your commitment is. If you don't ask your customer this important question, you could deliver promise-plus service, only to find out that your customer is unsatisfied with it. It's no fun giving extra effort, only to have it yield little or no benefit. Confirmation of acceptance by asking up front will prepare you for positive results.

3. *Deliver what you promise, plus something more.* Do a little better than what your customer confirmed was acceptable. By executing the first two tactics well, you set yourself up for an easy number three. You thrill your customers.

A critic might suggest that you are giving away profit unnecessarily here. How does the saying go: "Penny wise and pound foolish"? The return on this investment in the form of long-term loyalty shoots off the charts. Remember that it takes only a little to get a lot in return.

There exist a variety of ways to deliver the "plus" in promise-plus service. Pick one of these, or create your own:

- *Delivery Time.* Customers want their products and services as soon as possible. You may feel the same way when you purchase something. You can't wait to get your hands on it. Beating your agreed-on delivery time excites people.

- *Cost.* Your customers are accustomed to paying at least as much as was quoted. Frequently companies hit them with additional costs that were not previously disclosed. Charging your customers a little less than you agreed to will certainly light them up.

- *Quantity.* If you can't beat the cost you promised on a product or service, give them more of it. Giving your customers a little more doesn't cost much. It's easy and typically inexpensive.

- *Warranty.* Furnishing a slightly extended warranty at no charge provides promise-plus service and shows confidence in your products. You inform your customers that your products are reliable, and you back up your words with action.

- *Extras.* Throw in some extras. Perhaps you could upgrade the order to a slightly better model at no charge. Include some accessories or supplies for free. Again, the cost can be minimal. The gesture is more significant than the dollar value of the freebie.

To test the power of promise-plus, try it in your personal life. Call your spouse or significant other to discuss what time you will be home from work. Prior to the call, determine what time you anticipate arriving home. Then add thirty minutes to build a buffer. During the phone call, ask your spouse if your estimated time of arrival is acceptable. Once you both agree, you are set.

When you walk through the door fifteen minutes early, observe your spouse's reaction. It likely will range from mild shock to fall-on-the-floor fainting. Be prepared to catch your spouse on the way down.

The joy in your spouse's eyes will mirror your customers' reactions when you deliver promise-plus service. Something about getting more than expected lights people up.

Remember: Good enough . . . isn't.

Creatively Differentiate Services

Provide at least one service that is different than anyone else in your industry offers. This requires creativity, but the results are worth the brainstorming. The less differentiated your product is, the more differentiated your service must be. If your product is a commodity, your service can't be common, or you will perish—rapidly.

Tom Seitz and Ken Schuermann, friends of mine, recently started a new business called Top Shelf Bottled Water. They sell bottled water to businesses. Talk about a commodity. At last glance, there were approximately seven bezillion bottled water manufacturers. Bottled water is not the easiest thing in the world to differentiate. Everybody claims theirs is the cleanest and the purest. What else can they say? They can't say it tastes great or is less filling than their competition.

Tom and Ken have grown Top Shelf from a no-name to a dominant regional player in less than a year through creative differentiation. The sales reps deliver the water to the businesses at no additional charge. That is not different from some of their competitors. What is different is that unlike their competitors, they don't wear brown overalls or tattered jeans. Instead, they wear black tuxedos and white gloves.

What an impact. Do their customers perceive they are receiving high-quality bottle water? Absolutely. Does Top Shelf stand out from the rest of the crowd? Does Madonna? Everybody in town recognizes the Top Shelf sales reps. Their service is superior, and their attire acts as a constant reminder.

A little creativity goes a long way.

Surprise, Surprise

People love pleasant surprises.

Some customers have mundane jobs; they do the same thing day in and day out. Others experience frequent surprises—all bad.

A touch of thoughtfulness can brighten a customer's day. Let her know that you care about her as a friend. A pleasant surprise for no specific reason is a great way to show that you care.

A few years ago, I visited one of my key accounts. The person I had an appointment with, Sally, was called away to handle a business emergency. Her secretary informed me of the circumstances and apologized on behalf of her manager. I could read in her eyes that this was an unpleasant situation.

Seeing the opportunity, I went over to the vending machine and purchased a roll of Lifesavers. I wrote a note offering this gift in order to help her stay "afloat" during this challenging time. I asked Sally's secretary to give the gift and note to Sally on her return.

That evening I received a page. Yes, it was Sally. She informed me that my gesture was the nicest surprise she had received in a long time.

Many competitors have tried to get Sally's business. Guess what? I still do business with Sally and her account. And I will for a long time to come.

There are infinite ways to surprise your customers. I once sent an article from the newspaper on beer brewing to a customer who had just started this new hobby. A friend got Sean Connery's autograph for a customer who adored the actor. Another sent a bouquet of flowers to the hotel room of a customer who was out of town at a trade show.

To get even more creative, you might consider delivering a surprise to a customer's loved one. I was scheduled to go on vacation with my wife and kids to Tampa, Florida. Prior to the trip, I was speaking about it with the CEO of one of my accounts, Joe Broecker. He mentioned that he was originally from Tampa. I asked him if he had any relatives living there currently. He responded that his mother still lived in Tampa. His father had passed away recently, and his mom was now living alone. Some family lived in the vicinity, but she was lonely. His mood was somber as he spoke.

I offered to bring his mother flowers on his behalf while I was in Tampa. His eyes lit up. He said he would be very grateful for such a gesture.

Joe's mom lived just a couple miles from where we were staying. In the spirit of giving, I thought this might be a good opportunity for the entire family. My wife and children were less than enamored with the idea, yet agreed to it with the stipulation that the visit would be brief. One morning we picked up a fresh, beautiful bouquet of flowers and stopped at the bakery to get some fresh muffins. We brought them over to Mrs. Broecker.

I explained who we were and that the gifts were on behalf of her son. She was absolutely ecstatic. She invited us in to visit and enjoy the muffins with her. She gave the kids a bottle of soda with a special straw, which kept them occupied as we talked. We looked at pictures of her son as well as the rest of the family. I shared some flattering stories about Joe with her. In turn, she spoke of him when he was a youngster growing up.

Mrs. Broecker thanked us profusely for the muffins and flowers. It was obvious, though, that she was most thankful that we, in conjunction with her son, took the time to think of her. She hugged us as we left. The tears welled up in her eyes.

It was a rewarding experience for my family also. It took less than two hours out of our vacation. The feeling we had in our hearts was well worth this effort. The glow on her face stayed with all of us for the rest of the trip, and then some.

When I returned home, there was a voice mail waiting for me from Joe. He asked me to come see him when I had the chance. When I saw Joe, he was wearing the same look on his face that his mom had. The glow was unmistakable. I don't remember exactly what he said, but he didn't need to say anything. His face said it for him.

These are just a few examples of how you can pleasantly surprise your customers. The better you know them as friends, the easier it is to think of the surprises.

Perhaps the biggest surprise, though, is the reward that you get back from the surprise. My family and I never expected anything in return. As it turned out, our visit with Mrs. Broecker was the most memorable part of our trip.

Say Thank You

You have plenty of reasons to thank your customers. For openers, they write your paychecks. Whenever they purchase something from you, they are contributing to your compensation. That is a pretty good start.

They also refer other customers to you. They stick with you through product performance problems. Your loyal customers increase the amount of products they acquire from you.

Thank your customers for these things for two reasons. First, it is the right thing to do. To forgo it would be both self-centered and ungrateful. Show you care about your customers as friends. Second, that which is rewarded is repeated. If you want your customers to continue to do for you, reward them with special thanks.

Thank them immediately after their kind gestures. As each day passes, the value of the thank-you diminishes slightly. When you respond immediately, you convey to your customers that their efforts were so meaningful that you dropped what you were doing to thank them. When you wait, you imply that other things were more important on your priority list than thanking them. By the nature of sales, you occasionally expect customers to drop their work to do something for you. Show them the same response in return.

Here are a few ideas to thank your customers in special ways. There are as many options as there are personalities:

- *Coupon for a Free* . . . . Include a self-created coupon in a thank-you note—for example: a night of drinks on your tab or a free service your company provides. This shows a personal touch. A coupon works well in tandem with the next idea.
- *Night on the Town.* You know how important family time is to many customers, and you probably also know how hard it is to find baby-sitters. In addition to giving them a gift certificate to a fine restaurant, baby-sit their children. This has a major double benefit: Your family gets to know their family too.

- *Lottery Tickets*. Include a note with a few lottery tickets that says, "Thanks a million." Inexpensive and innovative.
- *Massage*. This is a great stress reliever that people might not splurge on themselves. It usually garners positive response from customers.
- *Sports Paraphernalia*. Sweatshirts, T-shirts, hats, pennants, mouse pads, key chains, and all the other products are more popular than ever before for sports lovers.
- *Team Magazines*. College and professional teams now have magazine and newspaper subscriptions that they offer to their fans. Your customer receives this gift throughout the year and thinks of you each time it arrives. Search the Internet by team or college name for ordering information.
- *Autograph*. Everybody has an idol. Find out who it is. Use your resourcefulness to get the autographed item.
- *Plaque or Framed Certificate*. This is a great way to recognize achievement. Plaques often find their way onto customers' walls, where they serve as a reward to the customer and a free advertisement for you.
- *Book*. You need to know your customer as a friend for this one. Giving a book appropriate to your customer's taste yields a moving, long-lasting impression. Write a short note inside the cover, so your customer will have a permanent memory of your thoughtfulness. Amazon.com and the other Internet bookstores can help you search for just the right book, and potentially expedite your shopping.
- *Items for Family*. Making children and spouses happy makes customers very happy. I can personally vouch for the merit of this approach. When I won the Sales Rep of the Year Award at Stryker one year, my company gave me a couple of gifts. The first was a gold Howard Miller clock. I certainly appreciated this generous gift. To my surprise, I was given a second gift: a Rolex watch. The dollar value of these gifts was similar, but the impact

of the second was tenfold the first. The gift was given to me...to give to my wife. The gesture was to thank her for her invaluable support to me and thus to Stryker. She was moved to tears. That remains the most memorable business gift I have ever received.

- *Entertainment Passes.* Some packages include two movie tickets, popcorn, and beverage. This gift pack again benefits the customer and significant other. Ballet, theater, and opera offer viable options.

- *Photographs.* Take a photograph of your customers with the new product they just purchased from you. Group photos are most popular. Frame it professionally, and give it to the customers to hang in their facility. For a high-tech impact, use a digital camera and e-mail the photograph to them.

- *Company Logo Items.* These are limitless: golf balls, oversized duffel bags, coffee cups, pens, calculators, hats, note pads, and so on. What they lack in creativity they make up in value. Every time they look at it, they remember you or your company.

- *Flowers.* These hold a dear spot in the hearts of many.

- *Flower Alternatives.* Baskets, balloons, and other items are rapidly increasing in popularity.

- *Cigars.* The rage lives on. Fine cigars and the associated paraphernalia offer a wide variety of choices and price ranges.

- *Food.* People love to eat. Lots of treats are available in stores and catalogues, and many low-fat options are available. Homemade adds a nice touch.

- *See Magic Step 2.* The "All Work And No Play" section of Magic Step 2 contains many good ideas. You could give any of these as a thank-you.

- *Thank-You Card.* At the very least, you should send a card. Keep in mind that a thank-you card may be the most you can give because some organizations dictate that employees cannot accept gifts. Know the rules.

The most important aspect of a thank-you, beyond the timing of it, is how well you gear it to the specific customer.

I once gave a hot romance book, a bag of O'Kee Do'Kee Cheddar Popcorn, and a bottle of moisturizing bubble bath to a customer. She loved it. She told me it was the best gift she ever received. I had learned in advance that these were three of her favorites. It cost me a whopping $19.76. That didn't matter. What mattered was that it was just perfect for her.

When Thank You Isn't Enough, Celebrate!

Sometimes a thank-you isn't enough. Then it's time for a celebration! This might apply when the magnitude of your thanks is beyond the ordinary. You are so excited about what you have accomplished with your customer that you want to celebrate.

Celebrations are often fitting when you want to thank an entire department or team. The ongoing trend in today's business world is toward team empowerment and activities, so the whole group often deserves thanks.

Here are a few celebration ideas:

- *Ice Cream Sundaes*—Easy and cost-effective. Buy ice cream in big tubs, and bring the fixings. This is a guaranteed big hit.
- *Cake*—Have the bakery write something special for the team on the cake. The thought means as much as the cake.
- *Pancakes*—A great breakfast idea. They are inexpensive and filling. The kinds that are mixed in the self-contained plastic bottle are easy and clean.
- *Lunch*—Either catered or at a restaurant. This is a fun way to thank the department and spend valuable time with them.
- *Champagne*—A classy approach. Bring the bubbly both with alcohol and alcohol free to be safe.
- *Beer*—The variety of domestic and imported brews continues to grow. A keg suits those looking for volume.

- *Balloons*—Fill the room with congratulations balloons.
- *Massage*—For stress relief for groups too. Pay a masseuse for a few hours and cycle people through in five- or ten-minute increments. The whole team will fall in love with you for this one.

You now possess a stockpile of little things to light up your customers. How rewarding it is to make people happy. Contrary to popular belief, nice guys finish first!

Can you feel the magic steps moving faster? The people down below are starting to look like ants. You are rising to stardom.

The magic continues. Your sales numbers grow...
Your customers love you. Look at them glow.

MAGIC STEP 5
HAVE FUN

Somewhere along the way, the business world forgot how to have fun. People take everything so seriously these days. The average adult laughs just a dozen times per day, while the average child laughs over a hundred times. What is wrong with this picture?

Perhaps there are good reasons. Leveraged buyouts, downsizing, work redesign, job reengineering, and the global economy are some root causes. Many customers and sales reps are still shell-shocked from all of these.

Stress levels have shot through the roof. In *Making Humor Work*, Dr. Terry Paulson informs us that businesspeople consume over fifteen tons of aspirin per day. Many are focused on keeping their jobs. Most are doing much more with much less. Some would say there just isn't time to have fun.

Quite the contrary. In trying times, having fun is imperative.

Consciously bring fun back into your customers' lives. Fun benefits you as much as your customers.

Humor provides an excellent conduit for fun. Most sales reps have a good sense of humor. Unfortunately, only a portion use this gift effectively. The skill is vastly underrated. In the hiring process, most managers have a list of key skills they look for in a new rep. "Sense of humor" seldom makes the list.

On the inside cover of my day planner, I keep this saying: Make Sure You're Having Fun with Your Customers. It serves as a daily reminder to lighten up, enjoy my job, and help my customers to do the same.

How Fun Works

To understand the rewards, you must first understand the dynamics of having a good time. Fun influences people physically, mentally, and emotionally.

"The neural circuits in your brain begin to reverberate. Chemical and electrical impulses start flowing rapidly through your body. The pituitary gland is stimulated, and hormones and endorphins race through your blood. Your body temperature rises half a degree, your pulse rate and blood pressure increase, your arteries and thoracic muscles contract, your vocal chords quiver, and your face contorts. Pressure builds in your lungs. Your lower jaw suddenly becomes uncontrollable, and breath bursts from your mouth at nearly seventy miles an hour."

What does this paragraph describe? Have you guessed it? Get your mind out of the gutter, please. It's the clinical description of laughter as told by Dr. Paulson. The physical effects of laughter are profound. It decreases muscle tension and increases overall relaxation.

Compare these effects with the following description: "It produces physical changes, including irritability, salt retention, blood pressure elevation, loss of essential minerals such as potassium and magnesium, erratic heart rhythms, increased fats and cholesterol in the bloodstream, and suppression of the sex hormones."

This is the clinical description of the physical effects of stress as stated by Dr. Robert Elliot in *From Stress to Strength*. Despite this contrast, the business world routinely chooses worry over laughter. Go figure.

Laughter benefits you mentally as well. People get enveloped in the stresses of their work and easily become overwhelmed. Pain intensifies when attention is given to it. People remain in this rut unless something interrupts the course.

Laughter provides a great distraction. It can derail the stress train instantly by shutting off the flow of stress hormones. Laughter helps you to keep everything in proper perspective. You are better able to keep loose physically and mentally. Humor helps you handle what otherwise might be overwhelming.

These physical and mental transformations yield emotional dividends. Your attitude improves noticeably. Laughter reverses the apprehension, irritability, and unpleasant feelings that worrying creates. Simply said, you are happier. Your patience and resiliency increase. You become emotionally energized. The train travels on track with a full head of steam.

Humor Heals

Does having fun really make a tangible difference? The answer is an emphatic yes! To support this assertion, look no further than your local hospital.

Norman Cousins had a serious, painful disease of the connective tissue. In his book *Anatomy of an Illness*, Cousins described how he used laughter to overcome his potentially fatal illness.

He once said that laughter is jogging for the intestines. Others have stated that a good three-minute laugh is worth twenty minutes of exercise. Surprisingly enough, given the choice, I'll pick the three-minute laugh.

Recently the use of humor in medicine has taken off. Many hospitals have active humor therapy programs now. *In Laugh After Laugh: The Healing Power of Humor*, Raymond Moody, Jr., states that "there is an inverse relationship between humor and pain." Laughter increases the production of endorphins, which act as the body's natural painkillers. Research has also shown that laughter can lower blood pressure and stimulate the immune system to help fight viruses, bacteria, heart disease, and even cancer. It is no wonder that people have been saying for years, "Laughter is the best medicine."

How does this apply to you in your sales role? Here is the connection. If having fun can catalyze the cure of cancer, it can assuredly help your customers overcome their daily problems.

For clarity, let's break the term *problem* into two parts: (1) problem with your product and (2) problem with another company's product. Gaining loyalty and success hinges on helping your customers in both respects.

At first glance, it seems that nothing is humorous about a problem with your product. In Magic Step 3, you discovered the Seven Magic Keys to Problem Solving. Using humor plays a role in one of the keys we discussed: to break the tension of the situation. The story of how Jim Heath from Canon overcame serious product problems with Toal Custom Graphics has a bit more to it. He shared with me how effectively humor functioned in that tense situation.

When he first spoke with Carol, the manager of the business, she was unusually defensive, angry, and serious—not a good combination. At one point in the conversation, Jim said, "Carol, I would love to come over immediately to fix the copier. However, it is highly likely that with my mechanical talent, I would cause the copier to spontaneously combust. While this would eliminate any further problems, you might be better served if I bring in a team of experts to fix it ASAP."

When Carol laughed, Jim could feel the tension release through the phone. Her anger defused, Carol's defensiveness dissipated. Jim had strategically used humor to pave the way to a successful problem resolution.

Humor helps manage conflict. It facilitates both parties in making the transition from confrontation to resolution. (Caution: Rely on your customer relationships to avoid picking customers who might respond negatively to this approach.) Be sure to reinforce your sincere concern about the problem and your genuine intent to implement a resolution. Nevertheless, allow humor to put problems into proper perspective. Realize that you are not dealing with cancer here.

Let's move on to part 2: solving customers' problems with *other* companies' products. I am confident that my products are clearly superior to any others on the market. As far as I'm concerned, a customer who is using a competitive product has a problem. Sometimes the problem is obvious to the customer. Other times, though, you may need to assist your customers to see the inadequacies of the competitors' products that they are using. Having fun can play an important role in solving the problems and generating new sales in either case.

Having fun works with these sales in similar fashion to current product problems. The objective is different, but the path is the same.

In many sales scenarios, some level of tension is in the air. Both parties feel discomfort. (Isn't that a great word: *discomfort?* My dentist uses it when I am sitting in his chair: "Tim, you're going to feel a little discomfort now." Translation: "Prepare for the worst pain you have ever experienced in your life.") Anyway, sales calls typically aren't as painful as going to the dentist, but it can seem like it for some.

Having fun also brings people's guard down. Some may take it personally when you ask questions about the competitors' products they are using. Humor lightens the mood instantaneously. Having fun takes people off the defensive, which leads to an open exchange of information.

A brief story illustrates this point nicely. My friend Maria Foster was on a sales call visiting with a computer specialist named John Garside in the management information services department of one of Maria's accounts. John was clearly more adept at communicating with databases than with humans, and Maria could feel the tension of this sales situation building with each tick of the clock. If Maria didn't do something soon, John would have completely retracted into his turtle-like shell.

Out of the corner of her eye, Maria spotted a Dilbert cartoon posted on John's bulletin board and started laughing. John's eyes grew large as he smiled a curious smile. Maria bashfully apologized, "John, I apologize for interrupting our discussion. I couldn't help but notice your Dilbert cartoon. That is one of my all-time favorites. Do you remember the one about...?"

Both Maria and John laughed out loud as they exchanged descriptions of their favorite Dilbert clips. This lasted only a couple of minutes, yet it drastically altered the tone and the course of the meeting. John's shell vanished along with the tension in the room. The call proceeded in a comfortable, relaxed fashion. Positive results followed.

Fun also generates a creative atmosphere. It is difficult to feel creative when you are wound up so tight you can barely breath. As Patty Wooten described in her recent book *Compassionate Laughter: Jest for Your Health!* "Humor brings together the whole brain, linking the logical left brain with the creative right brain. Several research studies have shown that after perceiving something humorous, you become more creative at problem solving."

What a great prescription to overcome problems and facilitate increased sales: Have fun. That beats the heck out of fifteen tons of aspirin per day.

Effective Communication

Professors. Politicians. Sportscasters. Advertisers. Entertainers. Professional speakers. Sales reps. What do all of these professionals have in common? They use humor to communicate their message effectively. At least, the best in each of these categories do.

Why do advertisers use humor to sell you products? Because it works. Humor and selling go hand in hand.

This is the remote control generation. If you are bored with what is on TV—*click*—you change the channel. *Click, click, click.* You channel-surf until you find something that interests you. If you are watching a movie on the VCR—*click*—you fast-forward to the spot you want.

When you speak with your customers, pretend they have a remote control in their hands. If you are mundane—*click*. Should you bore them—*click*.

In reality, your customers do have the capability to click you. Granted, they don't literally have remote controls in their hands. Yet if you do not interest them, they mentally click you. Their eyes are open, but their minds are surfing to a more interesting channel.

Humor grabs people's attention. It unlocks audience receptivity. When customers are laughing, they drop their remote controls. As entertainment icon Johnny Carson profoundly put it, "People will pay a lot more to be entertained than educated." For you, humor itself isn't the goal. However, humor supports, enriches, and illustrates the real message. It brings the topic to life.

The quality of your communication with your customers drastically improves when you are having fun. Not only do you capture your customers' attention, you also energize their minds. Better retention of information results.

Certainly this theory applies to groups as well as to individuals. In fact, it may be more important to put fun into the mix when working with groups. People are quicker to the clicker when they are part of a larger audience. The earlier you make the communication fun, the better.

Fun Bonds

It has been said that laughter is the shortest distance between two people. Laughter is the great common denominator. Everybody likes to laugh. Having shared a laugh, suddenly you have experienced something in common with your customer. You connect with a person. The phrase "share a laugh" is profound. Indeed you do share something when you laugh with a person. The friendship bond germinates.

In some cases, having fun may be the only thing you have in common with another. I have virtually nothing in common with one of my friends. Profession, politics, religion, hobbies: none is a mutual interest. But I truly enjoy this friend for one reason: We always have fun together.

If I am at a party with a room full of friends, I seek him out immediately because I can always count on having a great time with him.

Although I do not recommend establishing friendships based solely on laughing together, certainly this is a great place to begin. Reflect back on the section How Fun Works. When you take your customers from worry to laughter, you have done them a huge favor.

The Nightingale-Conant tape series *Management Excellence* cited a survey that determined the top three most admired characteristics in a person. Sense of humor, warmth, and honesty won honors. Customers gain a new level of respect for you when you make them laugh.

Use It, Don't Abuse It

How do you avoid offending someone with humor? When and how do you use it? The short answer simply is: Use good judgment.

Don't Abuse It

Let's start with the easy ones. Avoid race, sex, politics, and religion as subjects for humor. People are often sensitive about these topics and easily offended.

Your laughter should not be at the expense of someone else. Refrain from poking fun at others. You are never certain who knows whom. Sure enough, the first time you crack a joke about the secretary in the department down the hall, you will find out that your customer is married to her. This type of humor has a negative and opposite effect of what you are trying to accomplish. Laugh *with* people, not at them.

Use It

There are lots of good ways to have fun. Telling jokes is one tool that sales reps have used for eons. Many reps have a knack for remembering and telling good jokes. Some write them down because they have difficulty recalling them. It is wise to have a couple of jokes in your repertoire in case the situation calls for them.

It is essential, though, not to be intimidated by the stereotype that all sales reps are great joke tellers. Personally I do not enjoy telling jokes. I am not comfortable with it. You don't need to be a professional comedian to have fun.

Spur-of-the-moment wit is a great stimulator of fun. One-liners are typically funnier and more impressive than prepared jokes anyway. An audience knows that the teller of a prepared joke is rarely the originator. That person probably heard the joke from someone else. The originator of a witty line pertinent to the situation is obvious. The element of surprise enhances the level of humor also.

Some people just cannot resist the urge to laugh at someone. Here is the solution if you can't resist the temptation: Laugh at yourself.

Self-deprecating humor can be practical. Let's face it: Laughing at someone else is a lot of fun. You give your customers someone to laugh at heartily and safely when you make yourself the butt of the joke. When you laugh at your mistakes, you encourage others to be more open as well. People often exaggerate the ramifications of their mistakes. Laughing at them adds a touch of reality.

It is crucial to laugh at your actions, not your person. You work hard to establish your credibility and your reputation with your customers, and you need them to have confidence in you. If you laugh at who you are, you undermine this. But when you laugh at an occasional mistake you've made, you actually reinforce the image you want to project. Everyone makes mistakes, so it requires a confident, secure person to admit and laugh at them. It also illustrates that you correct your mistakes rather than sweeping them under the carpet.

What if you just don't have a good sense of humor? You have tried hard to develop one, to no avail. Do not fret. Humor is not the only way to have fun. You are creative in your own way. Use your creativity to have fun.

My company makes a product that requires about thirty minutes of training in order to use it properly. The subject matter is less than thrilling. It has cured many of insomnia. As the sales rep of the product, I am the lucky winner who gets to be the trainer.

After the first sleeper of a training session, I knew I had to do something to spice it up, so I decided to play a game with quiz questions and prizes. I explained how the game would work at the outset but kept the prizes hidden. As we went through the training, I interspersed quiz questions pertinent to the material the customers were learning.

We had a blast! They hung on my every word. Hands flew up when I asked the quiz questions. Oohs and ahhhs rang out as the winners received their gifts. One would have thought I was giving away new cars. Actually, I gave away company logo items like T-shirts, sweatshirts, duffel bags, pens, and coffee mugs, with each prize creatively tied to the quiz answer. For example, one answer involved refrigerating a component prior to use. The prize for that question was a cooler. The customers cracked up laughing. A little corny—maybe. Great fun and superior retention of the educational material—definitely.

There is an abundance of ways to have fun with your customers. Determine what works with your style, and go for it.

Humor Is No Laughing Matter

The bottom line is that humor improves performance. Enhancing communication, strengthening friendships, solving product problems, generating new product sales: All of these contribute to better performance results.

Throughout your life, you have thrived on self-improvement. From schoolwork, sports, musical instruments, and physical conditioning, to your sales performance, you have focused on making yourself better. To accomplish this, you have accepted and implemented improvement plans that have included studying hours a day, running twenty wind-sprints each football practice, playing the piano countless hours, and eating a fat-free diet. Largely these have been painful experiences. Eating a scrumptious rice cake instead of a chocolate cake? I'd rather be obese than eat another one of those sawdust-tasting wafers.

Who would have thought that a prescription for improved performance could be so easy and enjoyable: Have fun!

The Magic continues. Your sales numbers grow....
Make work fun, ho-ho-ho!
[Okay, okay. That was a stretch.]

Magic Step 6

Time to Win

Without _____, you would have zero sales.

Plug in a few words, and attempt to figure out the answer to this riddle.

A car. Incorrect. You could sell by phone.

Clothes. For you perhaps, sales would increase markedly. For me, it would cause the opposite reaction due to my customers' laughing too hard to buy anything. You could still sell by phone without clothes, though.

A voice. Sales might actually *increase*. Some reps would be forced to listen for a change.

Time. You got it! 0 time = 0 sales. Without time, you would have zero sales. Time arguably is the most valuable asset you own. There is more magic in the wand of time than any other.

Viewing it from another angle, if you had two more hours per day than your competitors, you would destroy them. More cars wouldn't help. You can only wear one outfit at a time. One voice is more than enough.

Time, though, grows more valuable each day. Stress is at record levels largely because there isn't enough time to do what has to be done. Volumes of books, cassette series, seminars, and consultants specialize in time management. Many of them suggest that you should eliminate the unnecessary work in your schedule. Guess what? You cut the fat out ages ago.

Similar to previous topics, this chapter covers what typically spans an entire book. I understand that you want the essentials. The fluff you already know and don't have time to see again.

Time is a dirty, four-letter word to most people. Time is in finite supply. Everybody has twenty-four hours per day. It would take magic to create more time. By mastering time in all of its facets, that is precisely what you can do for yourself and your customers. Time is your friend, not your enemy.

On Time: Be Late...Be Bait

Promptness is a good place to start in discussing the many aspects of time. It creates the first impression of the meeting. As you know, first impressions are crucial. If reps are late, customers eat them like bait. It is offensive to be late. Customers' time is wasted. As far as good things and bad things go, that is not a good thing.

People who are late broadcast to their customers that they are undisciplined, unorganized, and disrespectful. A meeting may last five hours, yet if someone is five minutes late, that may be more memorable than the entire meeting.

Amazingly enough, a high percentage of sales reps are occasionally late, and many are routinely tardy. It is hard to fathom based on the consequences.

Granted, it is more challenging for sales reps to be on time than many other professions. Schedules are unpredictable. You don't know exactly how long your appointments will last. Who knows how drastically traffic might delay you. And let's not forget those untimely, unplanned emergencies. All of these are reasons. None of them is a valid excuse for being late.

Here are some ideas to use to avoid being late:

- *Consider scheduling your appointments for a time frame instead of a specific minute.* For example, try "late morning" or "11:00 to 11:30" versus "11:00 A.M." This gives you the flexibility to navigate through your tumultuous schedule. Of course, the customer's preference dictates how specific you need to be. The better the relationships you have with your customers, the more flexible they are with the meeting times. Some may still want an exact time. If so, happily agree to it.
- *Build in a thirty-minute buffer.* If you anticipate being able to meet at 11:00, schedule the meeting at 11:30. More often than not, 11:30 will work out just right. Things typically take longer than you expect them to. If you end up having extra time on your hands, use that opportunity to review the objectives of your meeting, make phone calls, or complete paperwork.

Even when you execute this strategy to perfection, circumstances beyond your control can cause you to run behind schedule. Don't despair. There is an excellent way to handle this and actually come out ahead.

With as much notice as possible, call ahead to reschedule the meeting. Customers understand that unforeseen circumstances pop up. Rescheduling is nothing new to them. It is critical to use the term *reschedule* rather than *late* when speaking with your customers to avoid the negative connotations of the word *late*.

Here is the kicker: When you reschedule the meeting, build in a buffer. This is tough to do because your urge is to give the best possible news about your arrival time. Nonetheless, resist the urge, and build enough of a buffer to ensure that you are actually early for the meeting this time. Does this ring a bell? Yes, the principles you employ to deliver promise-plus service apply here too.

If you are keeping score at home, without this approach you have one "late." That is a big negative score. If you do use this strategy, you tally one "reschedule" and one "early." Respectively, that yields a neutral and a big positive, which cumulatively equal a net positive. Clearly you convert a potentially negative consequence into a positive experience.

If you easily lose track of time, an alarm may be practical. Some watches and pagers have alarms. Setting an alarm for the time you need to leave for an appointment can be a helpful reminder. It can also be a polite way to break up a conversation with a person who doesn't take a breath between sentences.

Response Time: Speed Kills

In the remote control generation, you surf from channel to channel at warp speed. Overnight delivery, fax, pagers, e-mail, videoconferencing, the Concorde, notebook computers, Palm Pilots, wireless everything. The pace of the business world has increased remarkably. Business has the need for speed. Hence, your customers' expectations of your response time have climbed to record heights.

Rapid response time is valuable regardless of the request. Many think that responding quickly is necessary only in a problem-solving situation. Some think pagers are purely for emergencies. False. Anytime a customer needs an answer to a question, it is an emergency.

Response time was once measured in terms of days. Over time, it progressed to hours. Today your customers often expect to hear from you in a matter of minutes. If one minute of time is lost, so too is a portion of the most valuable "asset" they possess.

It is imperative that you deliver. Why? Your customers love it. Put yourself in their shoes. You call someone because you need an answer. The missing information is impeding your progress. You have to wait for the answer as precious minutes tick off the clock. If the wait is too long, you may choose to move on to another project. Sure enough, five minutes after you begin the next activity, you get the answer to the first one. You have to shift gears once again, wasting more time.

When you respond immediately to customer requests, you accelerate their progress rather than hinder it and make them more efficient. You may even give them the opportunity to finish their work sooner and get home for dinner on schedule for a change.

Your goal is to set records with response time. Respond within seconds of a request. Give your customers a priceless gift: time!

One of the weekly nighttime news programs recently ran a story about orange juice containers, which have evolved noticeably over the last few years. The peel-back and fold-open version is long gone. A carton with a spout on the side replaced it. Once the top is twisted off, a tab is removed, and the juice is ready to pour. The tab itself has gone through several iterations too. Why all the changes? Studies show that a fraction of a second difference in the time it takes to open a carton can determine which orange juice consumers will purchase. A fraction of a second! Keep in mind that your customers buy orange juice too.

Mastering response time requires two things: technology and attitude.

Technology

A plethora of technological gadgets are available to help you. As soon as this book hits the shelves, technology will have changed. At the time of this printing, here are some great ways to expedite response time:

- *Pager.* This is mandatory.
- *Cell Phone.* This too is a must. You have to be able to return a page if you aren't near a standard phone. Give your customers your cell phone number so they can access you immediately. If the cell phone is not within reach, most phone services have the capability of transferring the call to your pager.
- *Voice Mail.* If for some reason you are out of reach by cell phone and pager, you need a backup. Most companies have voice mail. Also, many pagers and cell phones offer voice-mail options.

- *Universal Number.* Some phone systems offer one toll-free phone number to access a person wherever he is. The user programs that number to transfer calls to the best possible phone number at the time. It could be an office number, cell phone number, pager, or any device that is reached through a phone number. Using one number certainly makes it convenient for your customers.

- *Virtual Office.* Many reps work out of their homes rather than company offices. If that is the case, you need the technology to respond just as quickly as if you were in the company office. Fax, scanner, copier, printer, and computer capabilities are required. For cost-effectiveness, the first four of these capabilities can be combined in one unit.

- *E-Mail.* It is only a matter of time before having an e-mail address is mandatory. E-mail is the preferred method of communication for many busy customers. If you don't have one already, now is the time. Print your e-mail address on your business cards to add a nice touch. For access during travel, Palm Pilots now have wireless e-mail capability.

Technology will continue to change. The point is to use whatever technology is available to communicate with your customers as quickly and easily as possible.

Attitude

The best technology in the world is useless, though, if you don't have the right attitude. Your competitors have plenty of excuses: "This is too expensive." "I don't want to be tied to a pager." "I am not a computer person." Let's look at each of these.

The Excuse: "This Is Too Expensive."

There is no price tag on time. The money you invest in saving customers' time is well invested. Besides, you can do this cost-effectively. As a sales rep, you have the skills to negotiate excellent deals. Pagers are inexpensive. You can negotiate with most places to acquire the pager itself for free. The monthly service charge should be reasonable.

Cell phones are not cheap. You must be smart with them, or the monthly bill can go through the roof. Again, you can negotiate to acquire the phone for free. Shopping around for a good per minute rate is key. Digital technology has drastically decreased the cost of operation, and fierce competition in the cell phone industry continues to escalate, bringing rates down to record lows.

I average about $400 per month for my cell phone bill, which equates to about 2,400 minutes on average each month. I obviously use it routinely for business. Bar none, it is my best investment of money. Every minute I use the cell phone as I drive saves a minute of standing still at a pay phone. That translates into one extra minute face to face with my customers. My calculator tells me that 2,400 minutes equals 40 hours. Is $400 worth an extra 40 hours per month in front of customers? My five-year-old son, Taylor, has mastered a highly appropriate response to questions of this nature, "Duh, Dad!" Cell phones are a necessity for rapid response time and improved productivity.

The Excuse: "I Don't Want to Be Tied to a Pager."
With regard to the concern of being tied to a pager, I must admit that I felt the same way before I procured one. I thought it would be like Big Brother attached to my belt. Having used a pager now for years, I can unequivocally put your fears to rest. I not only tolerate my pager; I love it.

Your customers are going to get in touch with you one way or the other. Their needs are not going to disappear just because it takes longer to reach you. Rather, their problems will fester and grow uglier. The sooner you satisfy the needs, the better.

One perk of having a pager is the ability to use it for personal reasons. When I am out with my wife, it is comforting to know that our baby-sitter can contact us immediately in an emergency. My wife and children have the number memorized to reach me for emergencies also.

What hours should you wear your pager? What about vacation? Do your customers expect you to return their pages then?

I firmly believe that you should be available twenty-four hours a day and broadcast that message to your customers. That sounds crazy to some. In reality, it is quite sane. I have practiced this for ten-plus years. Customers use this method of reaching me respectfully. It has been years since the last time I received a page at an unreasonable hour. As it turned out, it was a real emergency, and I was thankful that my customer paged me. What took five minutes to solve that night would have taken five months to repair had I turned off my pager. This shows true commitment to your customers, and they appreciate it.

How fast should you respond to a page? At what point should you drop what you are doing to return the call? The answer is to handle a pager beeping the same way that you respond to a phone ringing. In answering the phone, you certainly don't want a customer to suffer on the other end through multiple rings before you finally pick it up. The same is true of a pager. The customer has to sit there waiting for you to answer the page. The only difference is that the customer is staring at the phone instead of holding it to her ear. It's analogous to watching and waiting for a pot of water to boil. One minute feels like ten. By responding immediately to your pages, you save your customers time and eliminate the impatience of waiting for a return call.

It is unacceptable to cling to the excuse that your industry isn't the type that requires the use of pagers. I have heard it said before, "Pagers aren't needed in my industry. None of the reps use pagers." That is precisely why you should. Using a pager clearly gives you an advantage over your competitors, and customers in any industry appreciate speedy response time. If you don't capitalize on this opportunity, sooner or later one of your competitors will beat you to it. Don't let the unthinkable happen.

I also give my customers my home number. This may sound a bit overboard to some. Remember, though, your customers are your friends. Do you give your home number to your friends? Yes. Could your customers find your number anyway? Yes. (If your phone number is unlisted for personal security purposes, use good judgment in sharing your home number. Safety is, of course, the top priority.) It would be odd not to give your friends your home number. Do your customers use it often? That depends on how close you are to them. The better friends you are, the more often they use it. I cannot remember the last time I received an unwanted phone call at home from a customer.

Having said all this, I do agree that there are certain rare times that it is appropriate to declare yourself officially unreachable. When I am on vacation with my family, my focus is 100 percent on them. My customers understand.

Nevertheless, I set up a system so that my customers receive rapid response time despite my absence. I change the outgoing messages on my pager, cell phone, and voice mail. When my customers call those numbers, they hear a message from me that states the duration of my absence and how to contact the person who is covering for me. The person I choose has to share my passion for customer response time. I return the favor for him when he goes on vacation.

Vacation is an exception. Otherwise I am open for business 24/7. You must decide on your exceptions. The fewer you have, the better.

The Excuse: "I Am Not a Computer Person."
Some people are scared of the technology. Years ago, that was a valid fear. Navigating through the DOS system required memorizing commands, and using the system was tricky at times. Today, using computers and Internet for routine business use is easy. It is a matter of sitting down and doing it. The concepts are not difficult anymore. If you need help, ask any kid in the neighborhood to consult with you. It will only cost you a Popsicle or two.

Your attitude about response time must be passionate. Waiting a few minutes to return a page should revolt you. Be obsessed with getting answers to your customers in seconds. Your customers' time is their treasure.

As the title of this section declares, speed kills. In this case, speed kills the hopes of your competitors ever having the chance to get the business from your friends.

Magically Make Minutes for Yourself

By implementing the other magic steps that you have discovered, you have already mastered the majority of ways to make minutes appear out of thin air. Every minute you invest in strengthening your friendships saves an exponential number of minutes in return. For every three minutes you invest, you save nine. For five, you save twenty-five.

You understand that with solid friendships, you won't waste time defending competitive attacks. The attack doesn't get past the first step. You experience the speed of new product sales in the absence of barriers. You gain the pleasure of new customers based on referrals from your current customers.

You have accomplished so much before you even started trying. That sure was easy. Let's move on to some new ideas now.

You have heard the sayings: "People who fail to plan, plan to fail," "Plan your work, then work your plan," and "Don't start your day, until you have finished it." I certainly endorse all of those statements. Without question, success depends on proper planning. However, what exactly do those sayings mean? They are catchy, but what would you do differently having heard them? Not much. I will breathe life into these concepts with practical techniques for planning and execution. It is indeed a balancing act. Most sales reps don't spend enough time planning. Others plan too much and execute too little. The following system ensures a fine balance of both.

P.E.S.T

P.E.S.T., an acronym that stands for Planning and Execution System Technique, serves as the core of your time efficiency scheme. Why the name P.E.S.T.? It's in honor of those nagging requests that occasionally slip through the cracks like tiny insects. Those pests will never bug you again.

Almost all sales reps own organizers, which come in various styles and brands. Costs range from $15 to $500. Some are bound in fine leather. Others are electronic.

The fact that so many people use these organizers is encouraging. However, it is amazing how few people actually use them effectively as a system. Sales reps are no exception and perhaps the worst offenders. An extremely low percentage of reps use them effectively. The planners become a series of independent pieces of paper bound in leather. Notes are written as if on scrap paper in no particular order. The type of planner that you own is irrelevant. A $500 organizer can be misused just as easily as a $15 one.

Both Day-Timers and Franklin Covey provide educational tools to optimize the effectiveness of their planners. Day-Timers offers the *Time Management* video, which is approximately thirty minutes long. In addition, its Personal Time Power seminar comes in either a half-day or full-day format. The Day-Timers phone number is 1-800-225-5005. Franklin Covey offers the *What Matters Most* video and *What Matters Most* workshop. The video consists of two one-hour tapes, and the seminar runs one day in length. Franklin Covey's phone number is 1-800-331-7716. If you haven't already used one or more of these educational options, I highly recommend that you do so. The content is excellent, and the prices are reasonable.

P.E.S.T. adopts some of the principles from Franklin Covey and Day-Timers, adds a few new ones, and caters these concepts to the role of the sales rep.

Address and Phone Number List
Keep this list in or with your planner for easy access. Listing your customers' contact information separately in file jackets or keeping it on a computer in your office is inefficient. The numbers must be quickly referenced from your car, airport phone booths, and other locations during your travels.

Monthly Planning Calendar

Note your in-person appointments on this page (see Exhibit 4). The calendar should be large enough to write multiple meetings per day. This is advantageous versus scheduling appointments on the Daily Actions page.

For example, you attempt to schedule an appointment with a customer in South Bend on Thursday, but she is busy. If you are looking just at the Daily Actions page for Thursday, you have to start flipping through pages to find another convenient day for the meeting. Instead, if you are looking at the Monthly Planning Calendar, you can quickly see that you will be in South Bend again the following Tuesday with room for another appointment.

Customer Zone Sheet

The object in scheduling is to cluster calls in the same geographic area to minimize driving time. Creating a Customer Zone Sheet helps (see Exhibit 5).

Begin by dividing your customers by geographic zone. Next, list them by zone on one sheet of paper. Insert this piece into your planner next to the Monthly Planning Calendar in order to have both pages in front of you simultaneously. This improves your efficiency in clustering your calls. Once you schedule an appointment on Tuesday in South Bend, you can easily choose from the other customers in the South Bend zone to complete the remainder of the day.

Some might proclaim that they don't need to do this because they know all of the customers in each area. The question is, Why waste time scrolling through your memory for customers each time you need to set up an appointment? Invest your time more intelligently.

Daily Actions Pages

These pages are essential, yet they are also the most misunderstood concerning their value and proper use. With the exception of your in-person appointments that are displayed on the Monthly Planning Calendar, this

July 2001

Sun	Mon	Tue	Wed	Thu	Fri	Sat
1	2 Proposal Appt./ Home Office LGary 1:00 Tietema 3:00 Canada Day (Canada)	3 Holiday ↓	4 Holiday ↓ Independence Day	5 Spiel 9:00 Morgal 11:30 Panos 2:30	6 Patchin 7:00 Clark 9:30 Ross 10:30 Hanley 1:30 Fleming 4:30	7
8	9 Hoffman 8:30 Lamson 10:30 Haskell 1:00 Ritsema 4:00	10 Beloutz 8:30 Casko 10:30 T. Free 1:30 Spiel 4:30	11 Coates 7:00 Hennink 9:30 Mitchell 12:00 Lunch Conway 3:30	12 Kennedy 9:00 Cincannan 11:00 Golf with Nawrocki ↓	13 Streett 10:00	14
15	16 ↓ Success Seminar with Ross ↓	17 Fager 8:00 Reigle 2:30	18	19 Pesterfield 10:00	20	21
22	23	24	25 Golf with Casko ↓	26	27	28
29	30	31				

Exhibit 4. Monthly Planning Calendar.

Chicago

Patchin Corp

Coffey Tool

Hanley
Electronics

Fleming
Production

Clark
Services

Ross Energy

J Streett Co.

South Bend

Spielmaker
Adhesives

Panos
Products

Beleutz
Molding

Morgal
Instruments

Casko
Machines

T. Freeman
Industries

Indianpolis

Hoffman
Electric

HaskellCo

Riegle
Technology

Lamson Corp

Fager
Inc

Ritsema
Organization

Grand Rapids

Tietema
Roofing

Kennedy Tile

L Gary
Supplies

Cuncannan
River

Nawrocki
Construction

Detroit

Michalski
Plastics

Mitchell
Lumber

Hennink
Transportation

Coates Brothers

WF Donnelly

Pesterfield
Furniture

Conway Tool &
Die

Exhibit 5. Customer Zone Sheet.

page acts as the map for all of your actions throughout the day (see Exhibit 6).

All phone calls, quotes, letters, and other items are included here. Each night, prioritize the action items on the list:

A Actions you must complete the next day.

B Actions that you would like to tackle.

C Things that you will do if you have surplus time.

D Actions that you will complete when you are back at your home office at the end of the day or the beginning of the next day, such as quotes, faxes, literature requests, and other items that require materials or equipment that you don't have easy access to on the road. Some actions such as comprehensive proposals may require you to establish an appointment with yourself on the Monthly Planning Calendar due to their importance and length.

E E-mails that you need to send. Once you are on the Internet, you can easily scan your Daily Action page for "E's." This helps you avoid the common problem of clicking off the Internet and later finding another e-mail to send on your list. Trying to connect to the Internet once can be frustrating enough during peak hours. Reconnecting can be agonizing.

Further prioritize the A's, B's, C's, D's, and E's by number such as A-1, A-2, A-3, B-1, B-2, and so on.

The secret to determining which action to prioritize first is to ask yourself this question: If I could do only one more thing today, what should it be? This forces you to think about the consequences of your actions. Consider the results instead of the activities. Avoid doing whatever you find easiest or fastest. Take action on the items that produce the most valuable outcomes.

What does this prioritization do for you? You have in essence finished the day before you started it. You know in advance what you are going to do and in what order. You see a list of five A's and know that you have time to accomplish all of them easily. You think about them

24

Tuesday
July 2001

	S	M	T	W	T	F	S
	1	2	3	4	5	6	7
	8	9	10	11	12	13	14
	15	16	17	18	19	20	21
	22	23	**24**	25	26	27	28
	29	30	31				

Appointment Schedule

8

June 2001

S	M	T	W	T	F	S
					1	2
3	4	5	6	7	8	9
10	11	12	13	14	15	16
17	18	19	20	21	22	23
24	25	26	27	28	29	30

August 2001

S	M	T	W	T	F	S
			1	2	3	4
5	6	7	8	9	10	11
12	13	14	15	16	17	18
19	20	21	22	23	24	25
26	27	28	29	30	31	

✓ Task Completed
→ Planned Forward
✗ Task Deleted
ᴅ ⊘ Delegated Task
● In Process1

9

↓ ABC Prioritized Daily Task List

	A₅	Call Barczak-Neptune
	B₁	Call Curtis ① TPS ② PP
✗	D₂	Send S4 Literature - Lambert
✗	D₁	Fax Taccolini
✓	A₂	Call Tom Meagher - Appt.
●	A₃	Call Scott Stephen - H.O.P.
	E₁	Bernice Nation - Tlm Pic's
	C₂	Call Sharon Brown - Board App.
	C₁	Call Dave Mezz - Trial
	B₃	Call Mary Sexton - F/B
	B₂	Call Darla - Demo CBC
●	A₄	Call Doug Ward - $ issues
✓	A₁	Call Art Hartman - Mgt Adv.
	D₃	Send Zak-Spreadsheet
	B₄	Call Dylan - territory
	D₄	Send thanks to Graham
	C₃	Call Reynolds - Bills
	E₂	MacDowell - New Computer
	A₆	Call Rohloff, Marsh, Jones
	B₅	Call Collins - ND Game

10

11

12

1

2

3

4

5

6

Daily Expenses

7

8

© 1998 Franklin Covey Co.   www.franklincovey.com   Original-Classic

Exhibit 6. Daily Actions page.

only once. You act on the most important items first rather than the easy ones.

In the absence of this approach, people start the day without a clue of what they are going to do first. They see a list of twenty-five things to do and stress out, knowing that they don't have time to act on all of them. After they complete each task, they review the list again and think about which item they will attempt next. They cave into the incessant urge to clean up the easy little things first. They procrastinate on the tough yet important actions until there is no longer enough time to do them that day. The same misery repeats itself the next day.

As you progress, check off the completed items. Put an "X" in the box to delete a task. If you call a customer and leave a message, put a dot next to that action. If the customer doesn't call by the end of the day, put an arrow next to that item and move it to the following day for follow-up. If, instead, you check this one off after you leave a message and the customer doesn't call back, you could easily forget the action item. This is how many actions slip away unfinished.

It is clear now how to execute your daily action items. How do the items get on the list in the first place? This is the magic that turns independent activities into a cohesive, self-perpetuating system.

Anytime you have an interaction with a customer, agree to the next step in the process: preparing a proposal, finding an answer to a question, or calling the customer back the following week, for example. Agree with the customer on what the action is, who is doing it, and the timing for its completion.

Immediately note this information on the Daily Actions page on the day that you intend to complete it. The operative word in that sentence is *immediately*. If you wait until after the sales call, you could easily forget. By noting the action right away, you don't have to remember anything. In addition, by writing it down in front of the customer, you give her confidence that you will complete that task.

Sometimes the next step in the process is the customer's responsibility. Even reps who use planners pretty well may be stopping short here.

The common philosophy is that the customer agreed to take the action, so it is her responsibility to complete it. She noted the assignment in her planner, so there is no need for you to record it in yours. Incorrect.

As much as you love your customers, they are human too. They get busy. Many are overwhelmed by their workloads. Like sales reps, a low percentage of them use planning systems effectively. It doesn't matter who forgets to do something. Forgotten for one is forgotten for all.

That is why you ultimately take responsibility for both your actions and your customers'. It is your obligation to ensure that your customers fulfill their obligations. Note your customers' action items in your planner. Even if your customers forget, you will remember.

Here is an example of how this works. Say your customer agrees to call you with some information next Tuesday. You note that on next Tuesday's Daily Actions page with a dot next to it. Next Monday night, when you plan the following day, you will see this note and expect a call from the customer. If you have not heard from her by the end of the day, you move the action to the next appropriate day for follow-up. Perhaps you put it down for Friday to give her some leeway. If you still haven't heard from her, you call her on Friday to give her a polite and gentle reminder of her commitment to provide you with some information.

This technique significantly affects your productivity and shortens the sales cycle. New product sales move much faster as you and your customers use time more efficiently.

P.E.S.T. is self-perpetuating. Once in motion, it remains in motion. You don't have to stop and think what your next step should be with a certain customer. You don't have to wonder what you are going to do tomorrow. The day is planned before you even get there.

See the Daily Actions page in Exhibit 6. Notice the number of actions on the list. It is not uncommon to have twenty-five entries on a busy day. If you routinely have only a handful of actions each day, you are either not working very hard or not using P.E.S.T. correctly. The self-perpetuating nature of this system fills your pages with profitable actions. The results follow.

F.A.R.T.

Question: What top three job tasks do sales reps dislike the most?

Answer: Paperwork, paperwork, and paperwork.

Paperwork is a pain in the neck, and it slows you down. You probably hate it. Unfortunately, though, paperwork is a condition of your employment, and you must do it. But you may as well spend as little time on it as possible. Mail is a primary source of paperwork for reps. Since handling mail stinks, let's name this the F.A.R.T. approach. This acronym stands for *F*ile, *A*ct, *R*ead, *T*rash. Is this crass? Perhaps. Is it easy to remember? For sure.

The best time to review your mail is first thing in the morning. Allot a set amount of time in your schedule. Attacking the mail each day prevents it from piling up and swallowing your desk. You can respond quickly to action items when necessary. If you let the mail wait, you could delay a request that needs an immediate response.

Minimize your time handling incoming mail. This should be easy to remember in the light of the name of this tactic. Time is wasted if you continuously shuffle paperwork around your desk. Using F.A.R.T., each piece of paper touches your desk only once. Do one of four things with it:

File. When you receive certain information—for example, technical bulletins, product support pieces—you know that you will need to refer to it in the future. These pieces are typically short and can be scanned quickly. Review them immediately, and put them in an appropriate file.

Act. Some items that come in the mail require action. Complete the action immediately if it's urgent. Otherwise, note the item on the appropriate Daily Actions page. If an action will take an extended period of time to complete, block out an appointment with yourself in the Monthly Calendar page to tackle it. Each action then becomes part of P.E.S.T. This gives you peace of mind. You are confident that the action will be completed in a timely, prioritized fashion.

In the absence of this technique, each action item you receive in the mail becomes a weight on your conscience. You know it needs to be done, but you have no idea when you will do it or how you could find the time. The pressure causes you to try to complete all of the actions immediately. The job controls you instead of the reverse. You perform low-priority activities first, displacing the high-priority actions.

Read. You probably receive mounds of lengthy articles and publications. You want to read some of them to stay current and credible in your profession, but you don't have the time. Designate a Reading section in your briefcase. In one compartment or file in your bag, keep the articles worth reading. When you experience dead time, such as waiting for an appointment, flying on an airplane, or eating lunch, optimize your time by reading. You stay current this way and never waste a minute. Take note of how many reps waste this valuable time flipping through magazines or staring off into space. Your productivity level dwarfs theirs.

Trash. This is the most underused of the four. You get far more junk in the mail than you may give credit. The natural tendency is to pile this stuff on your desk rather than throw any of it away. Soon there is so much clutter that the good stuff gets mixed up with the worthless stuff. You might act more cleverly by filing it or placing it in your Reading section. This is equally counterproductive. Your files become littered with trash, and you handle the paper more often than you should. Many reps save everything that has a mere 1 percent chance of having value later. The solution is to trash everything that meets these two criteria: (1) There is less than a 25 percent chance that you will need it in the future or (2) you could get the information from the source later if you actually need it. Don't keep things that you could retrieve from another source faster than you could remember where you filed it.

Reports

What about those pesky reports that you must submit to your manager: the weekly call reports, the monthly forecast reports, and so on? You guessed it: Note each item on the appropriate Daily Actions page. Say your forecast is due the first of each month. To give yourself ample time, write this action on the twentieth of each month's Daily Actions pages. You will not forget your reports again. Nor will you miss the strain of remembering it at the last minute and racing to finish it in the nick of time.

Right-Side-Up Scheduling

Even with excellent execution of these strategies, there are many days that you wish you had more time to get your work finished. The tendency is to stretch your days later and later. You find yourself coming home late for dinner routinely. Your family doesn't appreciate it, and rightfully not. Your family should be your top priority, not an afterthought. Before you know it, your family relationships are strained. The repercussions of this strain are not confined to your personal life. Your job performance suffers too.

The problem could be that you schedule your days upside down. You put a boundary at the beginning of the day and an open door at the end. You wake up each morning at about the same time, but finish each day as late as possible without being yelled at by your spouse.

Reverse this. (No, I do not mean that *you* should yell at *your* spouse.) Put an open door at the beginning of the day and a boundary at the end. This way, you preserve and strengthen your most important relationships. You place family first. Your guilt disappears. At the same time, you do not sacrifice job performance; in fact, you improve it.

When you have a long day ahead, start the day earlier. Early morning is the most productive time. Most people work upside down. Offices and phone lines are jammed late in the day and into the evening. Both are clear in the early morning. Your work is free of interruption.

On the other end, you must establish a boundary that is jointly acceptable to you and your family. My family and I have agreed to a boundary of 6:00 P.M. I am home and my work is put away for the evening at 6 o'clock sharp. Pick a time. If you live alone, you still need a personal life. If all you do is work, your sharpness declines. Balance improves performance.

Even if your work is not finished—and it never is—you still must stop at the cutoff time. The boundary is sacred and may not be infringed on. Initially this is challenging. Resist the temptation to finish that one last action item. The best way to overcome this urge is to remind yourself that you can finish it first thing in the morning. It will still be completed before others start their day.

To make this a habit initially, set an appointment with yourself at the boundary time each day for about two weeks. When you see an appointment written in your planner, you are conditioned to meet that obligation. Treat this appointment with the same reverence that you do your most important customer meetings. After two weeks, the habit of stopping work at the boundary time will be part of your routine. You may then omit writing this appointment in your planner.

I sense that you may doubt the realism of actually being able to employ this approach. What if you are "just not a morning person"? The bottom line is this: If I can do it, anyone can. From the time I was a kid continuing through college, I would slumber late. I routinely woke up at the crack of noon. The thought of getting up in the A.M. was out of the question. Now it is not unusual for me to wake up at 5:00 A.M. or earlier. I initially thought I would be a zombie at that hour. Surprisingly, I do some of my best work at that time.

Outsource

The last step in your plan is an easy one. If you aren't good at something, hire someone else who is to do it for you. If you stink at expense reports, hire a bookkeeper. If your letters look as if a fifth grader wrote them, use a secretarial service. You can work yourself into a frenzy trying to get these things done. Besides, they take you away from what you do best.

In the back of your mind, you might think that if you try hard enough, someday you will miraculously become good at these things. Don't kid yourself. I hate expense reports and will never be good at them. Gosh, I feel better already. I finally admitted it. I no longer do expense reports. My bookkeeper does. Do yourself a favor. If you aren't good at something, outsource it. Removing these stress headaches is well worth the investment.

Magically Give Minutes to Your Customers

Remember that 0 time = 0 sales. A similar formula applies to your customers: 0 time = 0 results.

Time is your customers' most valuable "asset" too. By helping your customers save time and operate more efficiently, you strengthen your friendships, and you improve their performance, which fortifies their loyalty to you.

Previously in this chapter, I spoke of being on time and having rapid response time. Both concepts save your customers time. It is worth repeating the value of excelling in these two skills. Let's now discuss a few more ways to give your customers minutes.

Saving Time

The most obvious is ironically the easiest to overlook: Your products often save your customers time. Your competitors focus so much on the other benefits of their products that they neglect to highlight the time-saving aspects.

Let's say that your competitor's product is a color copier. She focuses on the consistently high quality of the picture copy. The speed of the copier is next. She follows with the reliability statistics and explains how this reliability saves her customer money on service charges. Her product presentation is excellent...almost. She didn't mention the word *time* once.

Leave that approach to your competitor. Focus instead on how each of the product's strengths saves your customer time. By having a consistent, high-quality copy, the customer does not waste time fiddling with the settings trying to achieve an acceptable result. The speed of the copier minimizes time spent waiting for the copier to complete its task. As far as reliability, what happens when a copier breaks down? The customer's project is stopped incomplete. He must take the project to another color copier at some other location to finish it. The customer has to call for service. He has to explain the problem to the service engineer when he arrives. Tick, tick, tick...the clock keeps ticking.

Anticipating Needs

Anticipating your customers' needs is another great way to save your customers time. For example, in order to implement your new product, your customer needs to write a new safety protocol. In anticipation, you acquire a copy of a safety protocol that another customer wrote for this same product. You give this protocol to your new customer before she even thinks about starting on it. This saves the customer about an hour of actual work and several hours of procrastination and associated guilt.

There are lots of different ways to anticipate needs for your customers. They vary based on the industry, the product, and the customers. Your job is to look into the future to determine what those needs would be for each individual customer. Then act in advance of your customers' realizing they even have the needs.

Customers certainly appreciate the time savings. In addition, they are thankful for your thoughtfulness. You show them that you really care about them and their most valuable asset. Furthermore, you step up a notch in credibility. In today's business world, most people are mired in trying to catch up with the pile of work from yesterday. You impress your customers when you help them finish their work for tomorrow.

Organizing Things

Keeping things organized saves time as well. Anytime you can help your customers with organization, take advantage of it. You can do this in ways that directly and indirectly relate to your products.

From a direct perspective, your products often come with ancillary supplies and accessories. Your competitors expect your customers to figure out something to do with them. Take a different approach. Prior to shipping your product, determine a location and an organizational system for the supplies—for example, files, drawers, shelves, or bins. You know your product better than anybody else does, so it is appropriate for you to determine the best organizational method. When the product and accessories arrive at your customer's location, deliver the organizational items. With your customer's approval, set everything up in neatly organized fashion.

This saves your customers time twice. First, if you don't help your customers, most wait awhile before they organize things. It just doesn't reach the top of their priority lists. In the meantime, they suffer through the inefficiency of trying to find accessories that are piled in no particular order.

Second, once they get tired of wasting time searching for supplies, they eventually decide to organize things. It consumes their time to search out the right location and organizational system. Then they have to take the time to organize the accessories, which are now probably scattered in disarray.

In some situations, you can help your customers with organization in ways that are indirectly associated with your products. Things don't happen in a vacuum. When one thing is changed, it affects other things. Your role is to determine what those impacted areas are. Once you have done so, you can consult with your customers to help them organize their overall processes more efficiently.

You are the expert on your products. You have the experience of seeing the impact your products had on your customers' operations in previous sales you made. Sharing this knowledge with your new customers yields valuable time-saving results.

Highlighting Your Role

Whenever and however you give your customers minutes, highlight it. You risk losing the value of your efforts if you don't. Certainly be tactful, not boastful; you don't want to brag. The object is to bring to a level of your customers' consciousness all of the minutes that you are giving them. It really is as simple as saying out loud the key reason you are taking these actions for them.

Compare these two statements:

> "Darren, I brought this sample safety protocol in for you. I hope it helps."

> "Darren, I brought this sample safety protocol in for you. I understand how precious your time is. I thought that you could use your time much more efficiently than wasting hours trying to recreate a protocol that has already been developed. I hope this helps."

Obviously the second quote is more effective. This isn't bragging. This is just stating fact and purpose. If you are going to invest your time in these actions, take measures to ensure the greatest possible return.

Create Good Timing Magically

You have heard the phrases, "Timing is everything" and "I would rather be lucky than good." Truth lies in both of these clichés. Your competitors associate timing with luck. When they experience a situation with good timing, they attribute it to fate. On the other hand, you magically make your own luck. You consciously plan your actions to create good timing. Good timing doesn't happen to you. It happens because of you.

Before discussing how to do this, let's discuss why. Is good timing worth planning for? Is it overrated? The answers to those questions are yes and no, in that order. The right timing can clearly make the difference between a successful outcome and a failed one.

Think back to when you were a child. When you wanted something really badly from your parents, such as borrowing money for a date you landed, what did you do? You waited for them to be in their best moods before you asked them the all-important question. You knew you could kiss the money good-bye if you didn't catch them at the right time.

The same rule applies to customers that has always held true for parents. Most reps today have forgotten this tactic. They are too busy to take timing into consideration. They ask the big question whenever it fits into their schedules regardless of their customers' dispositions. Curiously, they are surprised when the answer is a big, fat no. They haven't a clue why.

How do you execute this strategy? Ask your customers. It is easier than guessing and quite a bit more accurate. Ask what the best time is to interact with them. This applies to the time of the day, the week, the month, and the year.

Some customers prefer mornings, when they have the fewest distractions. Others favor the end of the day, when they know their departure from the madness is imminent. The preference varies from person to person. You need to learn the answer for each customer.

From a weekly perspective, customers have much in common. After years of intense research and careful study, I developed the graph in Exhibit 7 to show the variance of customers' moods throughout the course of the week. The results of this study may not be revolutionary, but using them to your advantage is.

Schedule your important meetings toward the end of the week to take full advantage of your customers' best moods. Many reps make key appointments without consideration of the day of the week, even on Mondays. They would rather have a meeting on Monday than on Friday because it is more convenient, or they are too anxious to wait a few days. They would be better served to wait for a yes than to get a no immediately.

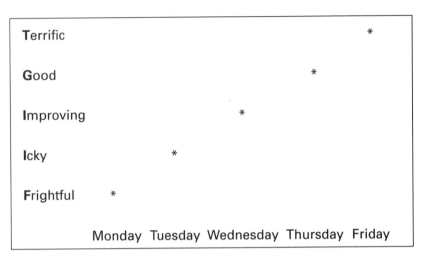

Exhibit 7. TGIIF Customer Mood Graph.

Take this weekly graph into consideration when you plan long weekends and administrative days too. Most reps take Friday off and give up their best selling day. Take Monday off instead, and you forestall your worst selling day.

Although the graph applies to most customers, it is nonetheless worth asking your customers if this is true for them. There may be other conditions to consider. For example, a customer could have a series of meetings each Friday. It is always worth asking rather than assuming.

Customers have their best times of the month and year as well. Businesses have cycles that affect this timing. Some have month-end and year-end reports to complete. Learning the best time of the month and year is worthwhile too.

There is a side benefit of asking your customers for this information. In addition to gaining the answers, you show your customers that you care about them. You are sensitive to their bad times and will be careful to stay out of their way during them.

While asking directly may be the best way, it is not the only way. Ask others who know your customers the same questions. Secretaries and co-workers are valuable sources of information. Their feedback adds insight to the answers you get when you ask customers directly. They may know your customers better in certain ways than your customers know themselves.

The last method to learn the best timing for your customers is through your own observation. As you make friends with your customers, you personally witness the good, the bad, and the ugly moods. Consciously recognize and take note of the best timing. Through the combination of asking customers directly, asking close associates, and using your own personal observation, you are ensured of discovering the best timing for your customers.

What happens if, after careful planning and consideration, you show up for the meeting, and the timing is terrible for your customer? Here is an example of what can happen if you handle the situation appropriately.

My good friend Tim Clifford had scheduled an important appointment with Mike Braun, a prospective customer and CEO of the business. Tim invited his manager, Carol Geer, to accompany him to the meeting. He knew Mike was on the fence about the decision, and he wanted Carol's support. Tim had hoped to gain the customer's commitment for a huge order. When they arrived, Tim asked Mike's secretary how he was doing that day. She responded that he had been in a terrible mood all day. She said it was something personal but didn't elaborate. She didn't need to.

Tim immediately rescheduled the meeting for a later date. It was the right decision.

When the meeting took place two weeks from that Friday, Mike was in a great mood. Tim gained Mike's commitment on the big order. Mike was pleased. Tim and Carol were ecstatic.

Months later, after Tim became a close friend of Mike, he learned of the reason for Mike's bad mood. Mike had been informed that morning by the family pediatrician that his son possibly had Hodgkin's disease. The tests taken the following week were negative. His son would be just fine.

You don't have to use much imagination to predict what could have happened to the order if Tim had gone forward with that meeting instead of rescheduling it.

Many reps would not have made the same decision Tim did. They would have been too anxious to get the order. They wouldn't have wanted to disappoint their managers. The inconvenience of rescheduling would have been too much. They would have forged ahead with the meeting and gotten a big rejection. It is worth waiting for a yes.

Ladies and gentlemen, what time is it? It is time to win!

The magic continues. Your sales numbers grow...
It's that time for your competition, home they go.

Magic Step 7

Get the Test Scores

This is the last step. Look at the beautiful clouds. They are below you now. Magic Step 7 seals your destiny as the number one sales rep.

Back to School

Bookends give books support, enabling them to stand straight. In the same way, Loyalty-Based Selling uses bookends, yet they are contained within the book itself. Magic Step 1, Get the Answers to the Test, opens in school. Magic Step 7 closes in school.

Reflecting on Magic Step 1, you imagined what it would have been like in school to possess the ability to get the answers to the test in advance of taking it. Certainly your chances of excelling would have been exceptional.

Let's say that you took the test. Afterward, you felt strongly about the likelihood that you achieved a great score. You were anxious to get the results. However, the results did not come. You never got the score and never found out how you did on the test. All the effort was for nothing.

This analogy holds true for most sales reps. They never find out the true scores on their tests. They work with their customers for years but don't ever learn how their customers truly feel about their performances.

They think they know how their customers feel. Were you ever surprised about your test scores in school? Remember the test you thought you flunked that you actually aced? Recall the test where just the opposite happened? Similar surprises occur in sales. Most reps just aren't aware of it. They don't ever ask for the scores.

Here is the best part of this school analogy. What if you were handed the correct answers and then given the chance to retake the test? Call it a "do-over." And after that test, you would receive the correct answers again. Subsequently, you would be given another opportunity to retake the test. This cycle would repeat itself indefinitely. How could you possibly not eventually ace these tests?

In the sales world, getting the score is as simple as asking for it. You learn directly from the source how your customers feel about your performance. You don't have to guess. Then you get another chance to deliver the best service your customers have ever received.

Why Do You Need to Ask?

In school, you didn't have to ask for your test scores. Whether you liked it or not, the teacher would give you the results. In sales, why do you need to ask for the scores from your customers? Shouldn't your customers give you this feedback on their own without prodding?

Perhaps, but they don't—at least not very often. Look at the numbers. According to Orvel Ray Wilson in his audiocassette tape series—*Guerrilla Selling—Live,* only one of twenty-six unhappy customers voice their dissatisfaction to that company. They do, however, tell numerous other people about their poor service. In fact, the average unhappy customer tells nine others. Twenty percent of them tell twenty people.

Of those who are dissatisfied, up to 90 percent won't buy again from that same company if their issues go unresolved. As stated in Magic Step 3, up to 95 percent will do business with that company again if their complaints are resolved quickly.

In terms of hearing good news from customers, that is unlikely also. As discussed in Magic Step 4, people don't compliment people as often as they used to. This applies not only to sales reps but to customers as well.

It seems that the most common time reps hear good things from their customers is when they leave their job. They get promoted or change companies, and suddenly they hear wonderful feedback from their customers.

What about those customers in the middle of the range, those receiving average service? You don't need to see a study to figure out that the chances of hearing from them are about one in a zillion. What would compel them to take time out of their busy schedule to call you and tell you things are average? Nothing.

The danger here is that these customers do not have strong feelings about you. Average service does not create loyalty. Whereas customers with unresolved complaints are the most likely to jump ship and go with competitors, those receiving average service follow close behind.

Now you know why you need to ask your customers for the score rather than relying on them to give it to you.

What Is in It for You?

What if a magic genie told you that she would give you magic powers to guarantee that all of your customers would perceive your service to be the best that they have ever received? That would be stellar.

Save your efforts, you don't need to search for the genie's lamp. You already posses the magic.

You learned from your customers with Magic Step 1 what it would take to provide them with the best service that they have ever received. Now simply ask them if you have delivered what they requested. You discover in this way where you might have fallen short and how to remedy it. They convey what you have done well so you can do more of it.

This process guarantees delivering your customers the best service ever. How awesome is that! How high will your sales numbers soar with customers that are ecstatic with your service?

Another benefit to you is direct feedback on your performance. Sure, your manager gives you an annual review, but what does she really know about how you are performing in your job? She travels with you to see you at work only occasionally. You take her to your favorite customers besides. She sees your sales numbers and infers how you are doing. You know that this is a good indicator of performance, but many other factors that are outside your control influence sales numbers. The only accurate assessment is through your customers' eyes.

The hidden dividend from asking for customer feedback is improving your friendships with your customers. The process itself deepens the intimacy of your bonds. When a person communicates feelings about another person directly, that is an intimate experience, and it requires real openness on both ends. Your customers truly invest themselves in you when they are willing to share these feelings with you.

Furthermore, when you are providing great service to your customers, this process reminds them how well you are treating them. Of course, your customers know it, yet this brings those thoughts and feelings to a conscious level. It eliminates the chance of taking you for granted.

On the other hand, if you are not giving them the service they deserve, you show them a sincere interest in changing your ways. Your humility and willingness to improve undoubtedly enhance your relationship in this situation too.

What Is in It for Your Customers?

With most good friendships, when one friend benefits, so does the other.

What if a magic genie told your customers that she would give them magic powers to guarantee that they received the best service ever from their sales reps? In essence, they too have been given that magic.

Any unmet service requirements will be met. The things they like they will see more of. Their pet peeves will vanish. Their level of satisfaction will improve assuredly. How easy their work lives would be if they had that same guarantee with all of their sales reps!

Poor service creates agony for customers. It disrupts their days and squanders their time. Their frustration and stress surge. Their service to their customers is adversely affected. Customers' performance diminishes. The opportunity to eliminate all of this pain is a huge benefit and relief to your customers.

Customers also receive the hidden benefit of deeper friendships. It feels good to your customers to share feedback openly with you. They realize the impact they have on improving your performance. As any great coach, mentor, or teacher would tell you, helping someone to grow and excel is deeply rewarding.

You Object

What would stop you from asking your customers for this kind of feedback? The biggest reason is fear. Even though sales reps typically have thick skin, it is not impenetrable. Negative feedback on your performance feels like someone just punched you in the stomach. Plainly, it hurts your feelings. It is personal.

Rather than face the possibility of receiving this bad news, most reps would rather not ask. They would prefer not knowing at all. This way they can pretend that the negative situations don't exist.

This is a mere objection. Aren't sales reps paid to overcome objections? All right, so how do you overcome this one?

Easily. Ask yourself one question: What is worse than hearing negative feedback? The answer is: Not hearing it. If you don't receive this negative feedback, the result can be a lost customer. Not hearing the feedback doesn't make the *problem* go away; it makes the *customer* go away. You still get the bad news; you just get it later, and with more severe consequences.

If you do receive the feedback, there is no question that it stings. However, once you have recovered from the initial blow, you can do something about it. You learn specifically what the customer is unhappy about. You can then eliminate the problem and deliver the best service the customer has ever had. The reward more than compensates for the initial pain.

Back to the school analogy, what if you thought you flunked a test? If you never picked up the test scores, what would happen? The scores would not go away. They might be out of your sight and mind, but they would still be in the direct sight of the instructor. Eventually you would get the feedback. It would be in the form of an F on the report card for the test.

However, if you do pick up the test scores, you learn that you flunked that test. Yes, that bites. Don't forget the special rules though. You get to retake the test! Oh, and you get the correct answers to all the test questions first. That leads to an A instead of an F for the test.

The other objection that you might have is time. You learned in the previous chapter how important time is. This project would certainly take time. You are just too busy for this. With respect to time, you can't afford to do it right now.

False.

With respect to time, you can't afford *not* to do it right now. A customer can dump you in a heartbeat. It takes mountains of time to earn a new one.

This process guarantees strong relationships with your customers. It prevents customers from becoming dissatisfied with your service and switching to your competitors. You lose no customers. How much would you be willing to pay for such a guarantee? What a wonderful return on your investment of time.

The amount of time you invest does not have to be exorbitant. With the help of the feedback sheet and cover letter examples provided in this chapter, that investment will be reduced considerably. Just customize these tools to your individual needs, using the examples as templates.

They Object

Your customers may have some objections of their own to your asking for their feedback on your service and performance. Not surprisingly, these are the same objections that you had.

They also are scared. They are afraid to hurt your feelings. Your customers know how it feels to get bad news and understandably do not want to deliver it. Certainly there are exceptions. You probably have had your head ripped off by a customer who seemed truly to enjoy the experience. The vast majority of customers, however, will be uncomfortable giving feedback if you don't address it up front.

You can overcome this objection in the same way you overcame it for yourself. Explain to your customers the value in hearing the feedback versus not hearing it. You diffuse their discomfort when you explain that you actually want the feedback and will not be offended by it.

The other objection your customers could have is time, their most precious asset. Your customers could perceive your request as a waste of that valuable asset.

As the song goes, "It takes time to make time." In this case, it takes a little to make a lot. This process surely improves the level of service they receive from you. This investment of time reaps dividends every day thereafter.

Being sensitive to this issue, keep the time requirements to a minimum. Do not pepper your customers incessantly with trivial questions that yield insignificant information. Ask a select number of well-thought-out questions.

Best Service Ever. . .Guaranteed

The name for this process is critically important. If you call it a survey, it's over before it starts. People hate surveys. They reek of wasting time. Companies often send surveys to customers. Customers fill them out and never hear about them again.

Questionnaire also sounds trivial and time-squandering, and *evalua-*

tion can conjure negative emotions for many. It reminds them of performance evaluations when their bosses told them all the things they were doing wrong.

Recall from Magic Step 1 that the process is named Best Service Ever...Guaranteed because that is exactly what it does. It guarantees customers the best service they have ever received. Instantly, customers perceive value when they hear the name. Wasting time doesn't come to mind. Positive emotions are summoned.

The actual form that the customers complete is called the Best Service Ever...Guaranteed Feedback Sheet. Both *feedback* and *sheet* are relatively innocuous words. The word *feedback* creates positive thoughts for many. People often ask for feedback and complain that they don't get enough of it.

The Logistics

Initiate the Best Service Ever...Guaranteed process in writing. Send customers a cover letter and the Feedback Sheet. Ask them in the letter to fax the Feedback Sheet directly to you when they are finished. After you receive the sheets, review them carefully and schedule appointments with your customers to discuss the feedback in person. If you have not heard from a customer in two weeks, follow up with a phone call to ascertain the status. If the customer does not want to participate, this is the time to determine that. However, if the customer just needs more time, graciously accept that. You do not want to rush the customer. This information is too valuable to speed through. Make a note in your planner to follow up again in a couple weeks.

How many customers should you use the Best Service Ever...Guaranteed program with? That is a tough question. Every industry is different and each sales territory unique. In a perfect world, you would use this process with every contact at every account you have.

This may not be realistically possible. The best solution to this question is to prioritize your list of customers. Then allocate an appropriate amount of time for the project. You may choose to use a block of time to do it all at once, or you may sprinkle these customers in over time. The approach is a matter of personal preference. Ensuring the quality of this effort is a prerequisite. With no sacrifice to quality, maximize the quantity of customers in the given time period.

The Cover Letter

The example cover letter in Exhibit 8 serves as a template for you to use with your own customers. It highlights a few of the key elements from this chapter. The letter mentions that there is something in it for your customers. Most people become motivated when they know that they will directly benefit from their efforts. They have an influence on their own destiny. In this era, those opportunities can be rare.

The letter also states that this process is for your personal benefit. There is no reason to hide that fact. Your customers would see through it in a heartbeat anyway if you did. Rather, it is helpful to say that it is for your benefit. If your customers like you, they want to help you.

Overcoming the discomfort objection is an essential component of the cover letter. You want your customers to feel at ease and open with their responses. The information becomes more valuable to both of you.

The letter covers the logistics of the plan informing your customers how you will proceed. Additionally, including a time frame facilitates action on this item by your customers. If there is no time component mentioned, odds are that it will get lost in the sea of paperwork.

Finally, you must give your customers an out. A customer may have a compelling reason not to participate. You don't want to alienate this person by forcing this issue. Also, people are much more positive about participating when something is perceived to be voluntary rather than mandatory.

The Feedback Sheet

A few characteristics of the feedback sheet in Exhibit 9 merit discussion. Notice that the questions are personalized in the voice of the customer. The customer knows immediately that this is not some survey generated

(text continues on page 142)

Dear Aime:

I would like to ask for your help. As I mentioned to you when we first met, it is my goal to provide you with the best service you have ever received. It is important to me to accomplish that goal for you. That is why I have created the Best Service Ever...Guaranteed program.

The plan is simple. In our initial meeting, I asked you what I could do to provide you with the best service that you have ever received. Now I am asking you to inform me of how well I executed your requests.

Aime, it would be of great benefit to me if you would complete the attached Best Service Ever...Guaranteed Feedback Sheet. The sheet is brief and to the point to minimize your time investment.

There will be a meaningful return on your investment that directly benefits you too. I will continue to do the things you like and improve those that you don't. This will inevitably lead to a superior level of service. You again have the opportunity to script exactly how you would like me to work with you. As the title to this plan implies, you will receive the Best Service Ever...Guaranteed.

Please be completely open with your feedback. The only way you can hurt my feelings is if you have an idea for my improvement but you don't share it with me. Not hearing it carries a far worse fate than hearing it. I cannot improve something that I am unaware of. You can be open with the positive feedback too. I promise it won't go to my head.

Once you have completed the Feedback Sheet, please fax it directly to me at 616–942–6680. I would like to set up an appointment to review this with you in person thereafter. I will contact you in about two weeks to see if this is possible. If you would prefer not to participate for any reason, I will understand. Otherwise, I will look forward to speaking with you about this soon.

Sincerely,

Tim Smith

Exhibit 8. Cover letter.

Thank you very much for participating in the Best Service Ever...Guaranteed plan. I certainly appreciate your help.

Please score the following questions on the support I deliver for you. The scale is 1–10, with 10 being the highest score:

1. ___ His response time is fast on my pages, voice mails, and other calls.
2. ___ He helps me to save time in my busy day.
3. ___ He is fun to work with.
4. ___ Interacting with him brightens my day.
5. ___ He partners with me to generate new ideas and recommendations that improve my business.
6. ___ He resolves problems quickly and effectively for me.
7. ___ He does the little things that show he cares about me personally.
8. ___ When he makes a commitment, he delivers what he promised or more.
9. ___ He actively listens to me.
10. ___ I consider him a friend.
11. ___ I can trust him.
12. ___ As a customer, I am loyally satisfied with his service.

Please answer the following questions with a written response:

13. If I were appointed CEO of Stryker, what would I do to improve the peformance of the company?
    _____
    _____

14. I have the choice to continue to do business with Tim Smith and his company, or switch to a different supplier. Does the service that he provides for me help secure my customer loyalty? _____
    _____

15. The overall service that he provides for me (circle one of the responses that follows):
    a. The best service I have ever received
    b. Very good
    c. Average
    d. Not very good
    e. Pathetic

16. What could he do to improve the service he provides for me?
    _____
    _____
    _____

17. What does he do well that I would like him to continue to do?
    _____
    _____

Exhibit 9. Best Service Ever...Guaranteed feedback sheet.

by a corporate conglomerate that will land in the infamous black hole.

The questions are quantitative and qualitative. Studies show that using both styles of questions elicits the most useful information. There are twelve quantitative and five qualitative questions. The length is reasonable yet comprehensive.

The quantitative questions reflect the middle five Magic Steps. (The first and last Magic Steps do not lend themselves to customer feedback.) There are two questions for each step. Based on the indispensable nature of Magic Step 2, Make Friends, there is a third question relating to it. The sheet includes one quantitative summary question (number 12). This format covers all of the crucial areas needed to provide your customers with the best service they have ever received.

In the qualitative section, number 13 allows the customer to suggest improvements in any aspect of the company. This is the only question that does not apply directly to you as sales rep. Why include this type of question if the customer's response will most likely apply to an issue that you have no direct responsibility for?

True, you may not have direct control over the issue. Nonetheless, it is your responsibility as a rep to ensure that your customer's satisfaction is high in relation to all aspects of your company. If your customer is unsatisfied with a certain part of your company, it is your role to do whatever is necessary to influence a promise-plus solution. The Best Service Ever...Guaranteed Feedback Sheet given to the right person in your company should offer strong leverage in accomplishing this.

Number 14 helps you to understand how much your customer values your service. The answer determines if your relationship is strong enough to retain this customer's business. It also acts as a reminder to the customer that great service and customer loyalty go hand in hand. The subtle message is that you are giving the customer the best service ever, and you ask at minimum to keep the current business in return.

The answer to number 15 tells you if you have attained your goal. The best way to ascertain the answer to a question is to ask it directly. This question is as direct as they come.

You would miss a great opportunity if you didn't determine an action plan for each customer based on the feedback you receive. The good news is that each customer does that for you with the last two questions. The customer virtually spells out what you need to do to achieve your goal of giving the best service ever.

"And the Customer Says…"

Trivia question: What was the name of the game show that the host's favorite saying was, "And the survey says…"?

Trivia answer: "Family Feud."

I have dedicated the title of this section to the fond memory of this game show and all others like it. *Survey* is a naughty word so I substituted *customer* in its place.

Let's discuss the results you can expect from the Best Service Ever…Guaranteed Feedback Sheet. Will the responses be what you predict, or will there be surprises?

If you don't know your customers well, you are in for a shock. If your relationships with your customers are strong, you will have few surprises. Most responses will be positive and on target with your anticipated answers.

Even so, there may be some exceptions. A few customers may surprise you by rating your service lower than you expect. This can sometimes happen when you take customers for granted, as you will see in the "Complacency Kills" section of this chapter.

Some reps might read this and say, "This would never happen to me." They may be in for some surprises. There is only one way to find out if it is happening to you: Use the Best Service Ever…Guaranteed plan.

Avoid arguing with your customers over their responses. Whether you agree with their feedback is irrelevant. Your customers are the only judges who count. You must listen with an open mind, and bite your tongue if necessary. The first time you disagree with a customer about her feedback is the last time you receive open responses from her.

There may be some positive surprises too. Sometimes customers feel strongly about the service you provide for them but don't show it. Some people aren't expressive in either their words or their body language. It is easy to perceive them as indifferent. Using the Best Service Ever... Guaranteed plan helps you to distinguish between real indifference and lack of expression. You may be pleasantly surprised with what you learn.

You may discover that your toughest customers become your most loyal fans. It may take a long time to win them over. It could be years and multiple Best Service Ever...Guaranteed sessions. Once you have finally given them the best service they have ever received in their eyes, you have loyal customers forever.

How honest will your customers be with you? Would you get more honest responses if the customers' answers were anonymous? I'll respond to the second question first: The answer is irrelevant. Although the quality of the feedback could be excellent, the value of the information would be minimal. Each customer's needs are unique, and so too is that person's perception of your service. Because the feedback would be anonymous, you couldn't possibly address the concerns of the specific customer.

Back to the first question. A small percentage shy away from open communication due to their discomfort with it. Perhaps surprisingly, most customers are quite open and honest in this process. The cover letter certainly facilitates forthright responses. Your customers understand the value of honesty in the process and often exceed your expectations in this respect.

Even with honest feedback, you may still see slightly higher scores with this direct approach versus an anonymous one. The same customer might give you a score of 8 on a question on your Feedback Sheet, where she might give you a 7 if it were anonymous. The bad news could be tempered a bit. This doesn't make the responses less honest or less valuable; it just changes the scale a tad.

You must take this factor into consideration in two ways. First, look at the relative value of scores as well as the actual value. For example, let's say a customer gives you all 9s with the exception of one 8. Looking only at the actual value of 8 might not create great concern. However, comparing that score to all of the others indeed causes alarm. The customer is sending you a message that she is not content with your performance in that area.

Second, mentally adjust the scale of the customer responses. Deduct 1 point for each score based on the lack of anonymity. That gives you a more accurate picture and produces a greater sense of urgency in bringing those scores up to 10. There is one exception. Customers typically give a 10 only when they really mean it. There is no need to deduct a point from the 10s. Take them at face value and celebrate.

Compelling statistics from Gallup provide strong support to the plan of bringing all scores up to 10. After extensive research, Gallup determined that customer retention is six times higher when a top score is given. Obviously nothing short of a 10 is acceptable.

Possibly the most pleasant surprise in this feedback process is how much your customers actually enjoy it. It is rewarding to praise people. Your customers feel as good about giving you the positive feedback as you do about receiving it. This is their chance to take a moment and thank you for your great service.

Many customers enjoy playing the role of coach and mentor. Seeing you improve over time based on their feedback generates a sense of accomplishment. It also creates a special bond between you.

Timing

How often you should use the Best Service Ever...Guaranteed plan varies by industry, territory, and personal preferences.

Once per year is the minimum acceptable frequency. Plenty can change in a year. A customer's satisfaction level could take a dive over that time span. The longer you wait, the greater the risk is of losing a customer.

Consider a three- or six-month interval with your least satisfied customers. This way you can more quickly determine how your action plan is having an impact on your customers' loyalty and your relationships with them. A year with unsatisfied customers is an eternity. They could be long gone before the twelfth month rolls around.

Sometimes a customer's attitude toward you can change almost overnight. The customer suddenly goes from warm and fuzzy to cold and clammy. What should you do? The best solution is an impromptu, informal Best Service Ever...Guaranteed discussion. Sit down with the customer and ask what has changed since your last Best Service Ever...Guaranteed review. Explain how important your relationship is with her. If something is bothering your customer, you want to resolve it immediately.

Here is an illustration of how this can work:

In January, I received excellent scores from Aime, a key contact at one of my largest accounts, during our Best Service Ever...Guaranteed review. In the middle of March, I sensed a sudden shift. Our warm conversations transformed into short and not-so-sweet discourses. Her attitude toward me had clearly changed, and I had no idea why. I racked my brain trying to recall something that I might have done to offend her. I contemplated how I could have failed her. I came up empty with this introspection.

I decided to make an appointment with her to learn the answer to this stumper. When we sat down together, I said, "Aime, I would like to have an open, heart-to-heart discussion with you. I am concerned about our friendship. Two months ago, I felt great about our relationship. You provided me with very positive feedback on the service that I have been delivering for you. Since then, I sense that something has changed. My guess is that I have done something to offend you. If I have, could you please tell me? I would like to apologize accordingly."

Aime responded, "Well, Tim, you are quite perceptive. Something has changed. I don't know how to say this, but here goes. I have recently suspected that you are having an affair. You didn't know it, but I overheard part of your conversation with your business associate in the hallway awhile ago. I heard all about your 'hot date.' Your wife was home while you went out for a nice dinner. Afterward, you had this great talk that lasted for hours. Like I don't know what that means. While this may be none of my business, I still find it immoral and inexcusable."

I couldn't help but smile. I explained to Aime that the "date" actually was with my eight-year-old daughter, Morgan. She didn't hear that part of my hallway discussion. I told Aime that sometimes I block out spaces in my schedule for one-on-one time with each of my two children. With our fast-paced family life, we found that one-on-one bonding time just didn't happen unless we scheduled it. Obviously it was not a romantic date.

We both laughed and felt a huge sigh of relief. I then had my wife, Cyndi, call Aime and thank her for sticking up for her. This call also served to eliminate any doubt that might have remained with Aime.

This misunderstanding, if left to fester, could have resulted in a lost customer and friend. Instead the concern was squelched immediately, and we were back to business as usual.

Complacency Kills

There is one potentially fatal side effect of creating excellent relationships with your customers: complacency.

It is easy to be lulled into complacency. It happens to your competitors routinely, and it can happen to you before you even realize it if you are not careful.

Complacency sets in when people take their customers for granted. They let up. They feel their customer relationships are so good that they can get by with less than stellar service for the short term. They believe they need the time to devote to gaining new customers. Soon the short term becomes the long term. This diminished service level becomes the norm.

This often occurs subconsciously. These reps may not intentionally decide to decrease the quality of service to their current customers. The change transpires gradually in small increments. Over time the difference can become significant and noticeable.

My good friend Dan Stark of the Spatz Corporation shared a story with me recently that shows the potential consequences of complacency.

On his first sales call at the Bowen Corporation, he met with Kevin Sullivan, the director of the purchasing department. Kevin's first comment went something like this: "Dan, you are probably familiar with the Hayman Company, one of your competitors. As far as we are concerned, they own our business. We have been with them for ten years, and they have given us excellent service. You don't have a prayer of getting any of that business. Don't waste your breath trying."

After Dan picked himself off the floor from that near knockout punch, he shared with Kevin that there was one product that Spatz offered that Hayman did not. Dan asked if they could focus on that one rather than attempting to challenge Goliath.

To Dan's credit, he didn't sulk and reduce his effort because he had the chance to sell only one product line to Bowen. Rather, as Magic Step 3 suggested, he blasted off with a big thing. One Monday afternoon about a week after they met, Kevin called Dan to inform him that the product he was interested in from Kevin's current supplier was on back order. He needed it for production at seven the next morning. If Kevin didn't receive it in time, production would be canceled. He told Dan that he would be in deep trouble with the production director, Mike McGarrity, if that happened. Kevin asked Dan if he could help.

Dan canceled his schedule for the remainder of Monday afternoon and Tuesday morning. He made a six-hour round trip to borrow product from another customer and then met with Kevin and Mike on Tuesday to ensure that they were comfortable with the use of the Spatz Corporation product.

This made a huge impact on both Kevin and Mike. They hadn't received service of this caliber in years. Needless to say, Dan won the business on that product line. The first seed of doubt was planted. Kevin began to ask himself just how good his service with the Hayman Company really was.

In time, Dan clearly demonstrated a superior level of service compared to the Hayman rep. He established and developed strong relationships with Kevin, Mike, and the rest of the staff.

In slightly less than a year, Dan had replaced all four of the Hayman product lines with his. Bowen Corporation entered a three-year exclusive agreement with Spatz. Dan locked the Hayman rep out of the account.

One of his best accounts had dumped him. The Hayman rep didn't know what hit him. Complacency is what hit him.

How can you avoid complacency?

Providing awesome service is as much mental as it is physical. Your mental attitude toward your customers largely determines the quality of your service.

Train your mind to view each account as a new customer whom you are really trying to impress. Pretend that each account is under attack from a competitive rep who is attempting to convert your business. In many cases, this may not be pretense. A competitive rep could be actively pursuing one of your current accounts this very moment, and you might not even know it.

Service can never be stagnant. It is either getting better or getting worse. Be hungry to improve continuously the level of service you give to each customer.

In tandem with your mental attitude, the Best Service Ever...Guaranteed process acts as an insurance policy that you are constantly improving your service to your customers. You spot hints of complacency and reverse the trend before it has a chance to worsen.

Never let up. Deliver the best service your new customers, old customers, and all in between have ever received.

You are now standing on the top step. I hope you enjoy the view!

You have the magic. You are number one!
7 - 0 = 1!

Congratulations

If I were to merely acknowledge the following people, it would be an injustice of epic proportions. Thus, I have reverently titled this section Congratulations!

Each of you shares the pride in this victory. Your fingerprints are visible on every page. Your passion ignited mine. The depth of my gratitude is beyond measure. Thank you for being the best friends an author could ever have!

The Smiths: You mean the world to me. You are my inspiration. Each day of my life begins with you and ends with you. Cyndi, you are the best friend and wife a man could ever have. Your wisdom and insight guide me through life. I have never overachieved more than the day I married you. Morgan and Taylor, you light a smile on my face each day I have the privilege of being your dad. Mom and Dad, your lifelong support, nourishment, and belief in me formed the foundation for this and all of my other accomplishments. Ned, Kathy, and Matt, our friendships far transcend our sibling ties. I love you all.

Helping Hands: This book would not exist without the opportunity and support that the Stryker team has given to me. John Brown, Si Johnson, Keric DeChant, Curt Hartman, Eric Teutsch, Pat Beyer, Bill Enquist, and Ned Lipes, you lead the best company on the planet. Father Beauchamp, Kathy Andrews, Terry Wybel, Marcus Buckingham, Tom Freeman, Don Mooney, Dave Mezzanotte, Brian Tierney, Todd Hennink, Jim Graham, Eric Graham, Bill Dubiel, and Doug Ward, you opened the doors to the publishing world that are usually locked shut to a first-time author. Dana Verville, Nancy Lambert, Carol Bowen, and John Casko, your brilliant ideas are sprinkled throughout this book. Chris Sommerdyke and Carol Ambrose, you gave it polish.

AMACOM: When you walk through the doors at AMACOM, you instantly feel the warmth, energy, and passion for your work. You make an excellent team. Mike Sivilli, your keen eye for detail, firm grasp of the intent behind the content, and overall ability to transfigure a raw manuscript into a first-class book make you great. Ellen Kadin, you have a precious combination of wisdom, drive, humor, and patience. You had the vision to see the promise of this book. Thank you for giving me this wonderful opportunity to become a published author. It is a treasure to call you a friend.

Naked Truth: It is easy to give good news. It takes courage and strength to tell an author that the manuscript he has poured his heart into needs improvement. Tom Seitz, Bill Dubiel, Jim Heath, Art Hartman, Dan Stark, Joe Broecker, Erin Byrne, Kevin McLeod, Ken Schuermann, Scott "Scooter" Stephen, Steve Deem, Brian Tierney, Mike Braun, Brendan O'Driscoll, Mom, and Dad, you shaped, honed, and enriched this book. Your contagious enthusiasm for perfection leaps off the pages.

Key Customers: Every lesson I have learned about sales I owe to you, my mentors and my friends. This book serves as tribute to you. Words cannot describe the value of your loyalty. Thank you all for being my customers.

Seat Belt: You told me it would be a roller-coaster ride. You were with me from start to finish through every twist and turn. When I was scared, you made me feel secure. You were always close to my heart. Whenever it went downhill, you led me upward to new heights. We shared sorrows and screams of joy. Thanks for being you, Mrs. Lala Seitz, a consummate giver.

All of you are Number One in your own special way!

SOURCES

Albrecht, Karl, and Ron Zemke. *Service America*. New York: Warner Books, 1995.

Cousins, Norman. *Anatomy of an Illness*. New York: Doubleday, 1991.

Day-Timers, Inc. *One Day-Timer*. Allentown, Penn. 18195.

Elliot, Dr. Robert S. *From Stress to Strength*. New York: Bantam Books, 1994.

Franklin Covey, 2200 West Parkway Blvd., Salt Lake City, Utah 84119.

Gallup Organization, 301 S. 68th Street Place, Lincoln, Nebr. 68510.

"Humor as Medicine." *Hope Health Letter 20*, no. 8 (August 2000).

Kinder, Jack, Garry Kinder, Michael Mescon, and Timothy Mescon. *Management Excellence*. Chicago: Nightingale-Conant Corp., 1990.

"Latest Victim of Downsizing Is the Lunch Hour." *USA Today*, Nov. 21–23, 1997.

Moody, Raymond, Jr. *Laugh After Laugh: The Healing Power of Humor.* Jacksonville, Fla.: Headwaters Press, 1978.

Paulson, Terry L. *Making Humor Work.* Menlo Park, Calif.: Crisp Learning, 1989.

Print Shop, The Learning Company/Broderbund, 88 Rowland Way, Novato, Calif. 94945.

Reichheld, Frederick G. *The Loyalty Effect.* Boston: Harvard Business School Press, 1996.

Tracy, Brian. "The Psychology of Selling" (cassettes). Chicago: Nightingale-Conant Corp., 1989.

Wilson, Orvel Ray. *Guerrilla Selling—Live* audiocassettes. Boulder, Colo.: Guerrilla Group, 1997.

Wooten, Patty. *Compassionate Laughter: Jest for Your Health!* Salt Lake City, Utah: Commune-a-Key Publishing, 1996.

INDEX